THE UNLEARNING SERIES

D1547794

UNLEARNING!

Leading Change Without Resistance

CHRISTINE KAHANE
DOUG KRUG

FALKIRK PRESS

Direct requests for permission to
ChristineKahane@ForUNLearning.com, FalKirk Press.

Books can be ordered for Bulk Sales through the publisher:

FALKIRK PRESS

InstituteForUNLearning.com
ChristineKahane@ForUNLearning.com

Cover and Book Design: Nick Zelinger, NZGraphics.com
Editor and Book Consultant: Dr. Judith Briles, The Book Shepherd
Illustration Art: Egon Selby

ISBN: 979-8-9893164-0-3 (Print)
ISBN: 979-8-9893164-1-0 (eBook)
ISBN: 979-8-9893164-2-7 (Audio)

LCCN: 2023920122

Business | Leadership | Change Management | Cultural Development

First Edition
Printed in the USA

UNLEARNING!

This book was written in its entirety
with Human Intelligence …
AI/ChatGPT was not used in
any part of this work.

AUTHORS' NOTE

The greatest illusion of this Universe is the illusion of separation. We are all connected. This is the core of *UNLearning!* and the central theme of this book.

We made this book for you to connect in ways you haven't tried yet, to create open spaces in your thinking, to allow you to find liberating structures for your business. It's a workbook on how you can become the leader everyone wants to work for.

HOW WE ARRIVED AT UNLEARNING

If you're going to *UNLearn* and get yourself quantumly untangled, we thought you should hear a little about how quantum entanglement got into our systems. We had an entanglement experience that started on the way to the airport.

Christine recalls:

We were tasked with facilitating a national sales team's annual conference. It was my first facilitation with The Institute. When I asked for the facilitation guide so I could study it on the plane, Doug said, "The Facilitation Guide is: We Show Up."

"Yes," I chuckled, "but where's the agenda?"

"They are the agenda. We are going to the conference and unlock them."

"You can't be serious?!" My heart started to pound so hard I couldn't hear myself think.

What ensued was a meltdown so loud Doug had to pull off the highway into a parking lot. He sat very still until I had worn myself out yelling about being ill-prepared, and how unprofessional this was. How they would judge us as slap-dash. How I wouldn't be caught dead in such a lost-cause operation.

He turned to me and said very quietly, "If you don't stop, I will leave you here."

I had a choice to make. The first thing I had to do was acknowledge that my fear was consuming me, and that there was another way. One I had never tried before. I just had to be willing to UNLearn everything I believed I needed in order to be successful.

Trust the Process.

Three days later we had mapped the Key Initiatives for change with the sales team, and they had committed to the change necessary to regain the trust of their stores, inspiration for their store managers and let's be real here: profitability.

What I'll always remember is how adrift I had felt until I surrendered and just trusted that we would know how to guide these two hundred people. We did it not by doing all the things I had learned to do: scripting every ten-minute increment into a twenty-page agenda. Two things guided us: believing the team had its own best answers and believing that nothing *separated* the team from those answers.

I've never been afraid to listen for the truth of a moment and speak that truth since that day in a parking lot on the side of the road.

It doesn't matter how much money, power, or authority the person sitting across from me exerts, when I tap into the intelligence we share, the illusion of everything that appears to separate us dissolves. The secret: We never take away someone's accountability by insisting we know better.

The solutions that come from this kind of collaboration are transformative.

But this kind of quantum solution can only happen after you agree to UNLearn what you think you need to have to succeed. You can get tremendous sustainable results if you let go of how you have to look and sound to be believed.

WHAT YOU STAND TO UNLEARN

Setting out to write *UNLearning,* we knew we wanted it to be useful for leaders who are frustrated with the current level of disengagement in their people. As in ... when even the best you are doing still doesn't produce the results you most want and need.

UNLearning is the wake-up call for returning common sense to common practice. It's a blueprint for you to build a direct connection to successful outcomes through your people.

To become that leader, we developed AMP. It's an approach to Awareness, Mindfulness and Presence, which we have been practicing for decades. They are the building blocks for connectedness and the tools against the illusion of separation.

The reason we created The Institute for UNLearning was to draw a playing field around our Mission: *a world that works for every living thing.* We come from a corporate America that works for those whose self-interest for profit and power has become the driving force for success at any price. In fact, people who work with this mantra are now being rewarded with staggering compensations. We wonder how many lead with AMP, and how many have agreed to trade in their awareness, mindfulness and presence for the illusion of it.

The illusion may sound something like this, "She's worth a fortune and laughing all the way to the bank!"

Questions came to us to answer for ourselves:

Are you fulfilled?
Are you truly, deeply happy?
How do you know when you are?
How can your happiness spread to those around you?

When we started asking those questions of ourselves, we were surprised that happiness was the central theme. So, we leaned into the questions and came up without answers we could live with.

We weren't happy.

We weren't happy because we had been conditioned to believe happiness wasn't something you were allowed to ask for or pursue at work. We were also conditioned to believe that when we made our first million, then we'd be happy. So happy, in fact, that we'd make the second one in half the time, and the third and fourth.

AMP DEFINED

Our work began by raising our Awareness, Mindfulness and Presence (AMP). And our mindset changed regarding what business is really for, and how to work with the people in it.

We also learned: Separating yourself from others works if what you want is more of what you have, while connection creates a playing field where possibilities become almost endless.

We knew that what we wanted was connection. Not because it meant we were going to feel good, but that we were going to get better at feeling. We knew that getting to the absence of separation would be where the possibilities would start to surface.

Fear had kept us from getting connected.

Sometimes, connection is the scariest place because connection only works when you're willing to show up aware and oh so honest in the moment, without any pretense, bravado, or know-it-allness.

So, to connect, we started getting clearer about how to become **present:** present with ourselves and one another, and then present in a room full of people. And then we started using our **awareness** of what was happening in the moment to inform our curiosity. And when we did that, the desire for understanding what it was like to be in another person's shoes took over any need to be the expert, the one who had all the answers.

We knew this for certain: the outcome that would serve the most profoundly was arriving in any given situation. This knowing made us **mindful** in all our interactions.

And we also knew that if we were going to be able to guide how to use the intelligence arriving in a given situation, we would need first to assume positive intent in everyone we met ... in every work project we took on.

What came out of those early facilitations was a rock-solid belief that everyone deserves to be seen, heard, and cared for. It's a belief we continue to stand by because we see staggering, positive results in people when they are seen, heard and engage as a result. Our belief became the grounding for what we now call The UNLearning Factor.

HOW DO YOU KNOW UNLEARNING IS FOR YOU?

So many of the calls we receive come from leaders facing chronic frustration. They've been told they are doing all the right things, yet they continue to struggle with never-ending disengagement. Change is only possible if the people charged with implementing change are *engaged*.

Are your people engaged?

How *do* you lead change without the resistance commonly associated with it?

Within these pages, we've captured the essence of the latest of what's working and what's not in our 30-plus years of supporting leaders. We've taken them from resistant to resilient, from conflicted to connected, and from high maintenance to super-high performance.

The UNLearning Factor is a nondisruptive creative process where stress and effort are nominal for engaged participants.

- Your takeaways include two elements. The first:
  To give you the lost steps for leading change,
  large or small. The AMP It Up UNLearning Lab
  that concludes each chapter is an opportunity
  for you and your teams to personally experience
  the benefits of our proven transformation-in-
  thinking process.

- The second: To open the path to your own
  UNLearning. Think of it as a journey, not a
  destination. The benefits you reap will last you,
  your teams, and your company a lifetime.

We build all our facilitation work on this premise: There are only two things going on in the Universe. There's either a move toward an expression of respect and caring, or there's a cry for it.

When you resist either, you are barricading yourself from the one thing that makes change possible: Change that comes with less stress and effort. And change for a world that works for every living thing.

Are you ready to live in the questions?

Christine and *Doug*

CONTENTS

SECTION I
THE CORE OF UNLEARNING

You've heard it again and again ... survival of the fittest, bootstrap it, do what it takes to get ahead. At The Institute for UNLearning our belief is that it's not necessarily the strongest of the species that wins, or the ones with the highest IQs, but the ones who integrate their IQ (Intelligence Quotient), and EQ (Emotional Intelligence), in the service of being adaptable. Your response to change will make you or break you. Literally.

It can be tempting to skip this section and head straight to the UNLearning Factor 5-steps. But, without a clear sense of how to harness your awareness, and what it gives you, in six months you'll likely wind up back where you started.

We encourage you to take advantage of these pages to gain a solid understanding of how to keep discovering who you are and what you're about. In these chapters you will hone what drives you, and how to move through old patterns of leadership that don't serve you or your teams any longer. You'll have an excellent context for how you can use The UNLearning Factor in Section II to build your leadership capacity.

1

Awareness

The Key to Leading Change without Resistance

It is awareness that focuses our attention and shapes our intentions. Awareness opens the door to *UNLearning.*

Cultivating present moment awareness is the radical source to all creative endeavors. Direct your awareness and you will direct energy. Direct energy and you will direct any choice you are manifesting.

BRING AWARENESS TO LIFE FIRST, THEN LEAD CHANGE WITHOUT RESISTANCE

Today, what is the biggest issue keeping CEOs up at night?

They can't get their workforce to innovate. But, according to statistics provided by The Muse, a company who matches workers with companies that share their values and needs, in its 2023 Survey, only two out of ten CEOs have any strategy in place to engage their workers in innovative practices. Their workforce innovators leave for greener pastures.

When we work with a team, we spend a good deal of time bringing them into awareness of their core belief systems, the ones that keep them bound to working harder at what keeps proving it isn't working. One of the most telling results is years of diminished intrinsic rewards come from the work you don't get paid for but that fulfill you beyond reason. Your passions.

On the other hand, awareness looks like release, like letting go, an exhale, an *aha,* and it's captivating because it's full of energy. You can feel it in the room. It literally heats up. Voices get louder and more animated. People jump to their feet and start gesticulating to one another. They're showing how their awareness *feels.*

The more moments of presence you can show up for, the more *momentum* you are able to build. Momentum is fuel for innovation. And innovation isn't anything more than a continual streaming of moment-to-moment awareness.

That string of moments is referred to as *Presencing.* It's the act of being present from one instant to the next and having awareness of and paying attention to what is showing up in those instances.

We are not the inventors of *Presencing.* Theory U at MIT has a Presencing Institute (PI), that is dedicated to its practice for global transformation

If you take nothing else from this book, take this: Your competitive edge in the shifting sands of global markets hinges on your capacity for generating AMP.

There is plenty to do for this state to exist. The first, and where we concentrate most of our work at The Institute, is in releasing, or UNLearning, any belief or activity that is preventing you from being in *present moment awareness.*

In rooms of executives and managers, salespeople, and C-suite leaders, we've repeatedly witnessed the light go on over people's heads as their bodies acknowledge the way they've always operated. As their awareness increases, they recognize the damage of autopilot and how it has held them and their organizations back from collaboration, innovation, and sustainable growth.

That light going on in you is the genius moment—*your* genius moment. The door opens. At the same moment, an alternative way has been grasped. It's like watching a light switch being flipped on. In *present moment awareness*, time expands. You know that you don't need an instant solution. Spaciousness moves into your core. And, in that stillness, you feel curious. *What else can I do ... so that we can do more of what works best?*

Doug has a great term for this experience. He calls it your *come-from,* which means "stop all the *doing* and focus on the *being."*

This movement into awareness is the brave act of getting unstuck. You are getting yourself out of the groove that produces the same result no matter how hard you work.

As the leader, you need to let your teams have the power. What does it feel like to be in a room where your team has the power?

We worked with a group who had been managed by a leader who believed his team was too stupid to understand his genius. He bragged about his achievements, his accolades, the people he knew and how the team would likely never amount to anything. Often, he was unreachable in the summer. He was at his lake house.

When we suggested it might be time for him to move to his lake house permanently, he took his retirement without a backward glance.

The new leader had a different idea. He asked us to join him to facilitate soon after he took over. It turned into a series of meetings with his ten department heads (the management team) who were given a voice in what they thought was working, and what they thought needed changing.

The new leader was present at every meeting: never taking a phone call; never monitoring his cell phone; and never leaving for "something more important" than what was transpiring right in that room. He listened to every word.

Some issues he was able to address on the spot. Changes were made in the room. Some issues he needed to deliberate with senior management. What he promised: No challenge or issue would go unheeded.

He kept his promise.

His management team bonded to such a degree through the process, they routinely find solutions to issues that come up as part of daily operations. In other words, issues aren't a demonstration of poor performance or mismanagement. Issues are a keystone to metamorphosis, or what we refer to as Continuous Renewal Economics™.

Today, as a result of liberating cultural structures, the team and company are operating at close to 200% year over year since that shift.

> *We decline to work with any group who wants us to come in as experts with all the answers and lists of what-to-do's.*

Once you and your team agree to let go of whatever beliefs you have, you start telling your truth ... about everything. It's catching! When one team member starts sharing, others hop on the bandwagon. And soon you are

challenging yourself and one another to change what's
not working.

Our job is to turn you and your team toward your own
best answers and to recognize them as that—your own!
When that starts happening look out. The whole playing field
will shift. Present-moment awareness has your team *engaged*.

When your team is engaged, a natural shift takes place.
It turns collective attention to what's working now, and then,
what new ideas can help make it work even better. Bars are
raised, limits set higher, good ideas are willing to be scrapped
in favor of new and better ones.

Now you've got innovation on your hands. If you give
your team permission to break what it made today in favor
of what it can imagine tomorrow, you've got massively brave
innovation. Very few companies are set up to do this. If you
have an R&D department, this is a great place for it to move
into this space.

And all you must do as the leader is to be **aware.** Be
aware of what's held your company back and get out of your
team's way.

It sounds simple … right? What could possibly go wrong?
Let us count the ways!

WHAT IT TAKES TO BECOME AWARE

Maybe the best way to shine some light on what it means to
become aware is to talk about what awareness is not.

A core belief we have at The Institute is that we decline to
work with any group by coming in as the experts with all
their answers and lists of what-to-dos. It is the antithesis of
present-moment awareness because it presumes that the
contracted folks in the front of the room have all those

answers. So your people become passive and move to autopilot, or worse, to resistance mode.

Whether they are telling you or not, your people recognize this type of information delivery as just more content being shoved at them, which they will be tasked with integrating. Is it any wonder 85% of workers are disengaged? Gallup research published these updated results in July 2023.

[*Your people resist* **being** *changed.*]

We had a client whose leadership team called us in before a big off-site event that we would be keynoting. Two enormous binders were dropped on the table in front of us, and one leader said, "This is the curriculum for our sales teams. We call them the dump trucks." Then they laughed their heads off. Was it any wonder that they had over a 50% turnover in their frontline sales teams across their 250 stores … annually? The cost to hire and train each year was prohibitive.

What did we do with the binders? We politely moved them aside and covered them with our coats.

If a group is ready to transition into UNLearning, the only purpose for bringing in the dump trucks is to remove the thinking that made them in the first place and use them as doorstops. We knew what was in front of us. The people who had put the dump truck binders together believed *they* had to be the ones with *all* the answers.

So what does it take to become aware? How do you make it happen? It's how you are feeling in this here and now moment, not what you're thinking or judging. If you can settle into that feeling and just be with it without any judgment, you are in present-moment awareness.

At a recent facilitation we conducted, a participant told a story I will always remember. She spoke with passion and joy, wanting to share her awareness through an experience.

My son cried with rage and frustration doing his homework last night. It happened right before he learned a big new thing.

It was so scary watching him. He huffed and threw his tablet into the sofa, got up and stamped around the room, screamed that Latin was stupid and he hated it and hated me for making him do it. And then he collapsed and sobbed. But then he stopped, picked up his tablet, flopped onto the sofa and didn't look up for an hour. Last night, my son translated two pages of Latin that was required for his class by himself. He's ten!

She had witnessed her son shift his mindset in order to learn Latin. It is what we call *real-eyes-ation,* and it had come through his embodied awareness that came online through his emotional surge. It was like an alarm in his system went off ... signaling change. He now saw with *fresh eyes.*

What comes to mind when you think of having fresh eyes?

The room cheered. They were with her. No doubt, many members of the team could share similar breakthrough stories. We witnessed the collective working organically to be one-with. It's the primary ingredient for any collaboration, and most certainly for innovation to occur.

We sensed a collective awareness in the room. What the room was becoming aware of was that it wasn't until her son, so vulnerable, so frustrated, just *surrendered* to what was wanting to happen that he was able to break through. First, he gave up. He released. He let go of the way he saw himself having to be so he could learn.

It is very hard to learn new things. It is very hard to live in new patterns. Because it is very hard to let go of what you are convinced you know for sure. Being open-minded is sometimes dangerous. Sometimes it hurts you. Sometimes it feeds you.

And here is where the light came on as she spoke: an instantaneous awareness that great change comes when you connect knowledge with your emotions. And it can happen in a nanosecond.

It is a perfect example of how strong your brain is. How it is wired to protect you from new information that you don't understand or could be dangerous. You protect yourself from things you don't know because those things might be dangerous. They might be incorrect. They might change you in ways that you cannot reverse. If you are like most, you don't like the unknown or uncertainty.

At The Institute we think of the moment of your being present as having fresh eyes on anything or anyone with whom you are engaged. Fresh—childlike, without any judgment, just the pure experience of breathing in and breathing out. Nothing to do, nowhere to go. Stillness. And then, slipping into a way of seeing that has everything around you falling together. Connected.

[*Your thoughts matter.*]

Here's a secret: You don't have to be ten to see with fresh eyes. In fact, if you can do it more often, the people around you will start doing more of it. A team seeing with fresh eyes is generating so much trust that they are capable of innovating in ways they may never have imagined.

How do you know when to let go?

When you experience an alternative where you let go of the way you've always done it, you expand your playing field. In quantum theory that place is called the Zero Point Field, where thoughts become matter. Energy that has been held back by your limiting beliefs, flows into your system. It changes your chemical balance: You feel tingles, heat, butterflies, and get out of breath. Your thoughts are literally *becoming*. They are becoming material (matter) as you sense the possibilities of how to manifest them.

In short, your thoughts matter.

In our facilitations, we've watched energy flow into one person, then spread to one person after another, until the team is vibrating with energy. It's the energy of possibility dependent on trust between individuals in the group. We see it as a raised level of collaboration in the room. People are animated. They gesticulate. They raise their voices. They laugh.

They leave the meeting and take that vibration—the awareness alive in their bodies—back to their departments, partners, communities. They get collaborative. Change happens. You get the picture.

That feeling in the body when your *UNLearn* signals are alerting you that change is occurring. Often it is sensed as shaking. We've heard clients say that they feel shaky, that their voices tremble.

Once a change is being registered in the body, your job is to lean in, breathe with it, so you can begin to trust it. What you will learn as you experience your body's messages more frequently—like shaking when you are speaking your truth—is that you *can* trust the somatic responses coming from what you are UNLearning.

The more you trust what your body's messages are telling you, the more confidence in your ability to adapt to any situation will grow, without having it all figured out ahead of time. Your growth will be exponential. And because you are built for connection, it will start working in all areas of your life.

AMP It Up | UNLearning Lab

1. What is one area of your leadership where you feel most stuck? Do you associate the stuckness with a sensation in your body? What is it, and how will you recognize it in the future?

2. What's one thing you are willing to trust because your body wisdom is telling you it's "okay"? Maybe something or someone you haven't been willing to trust in the past?

Key UNLearnings

✓ 85% of the global workforce is disengaged.

✓ Bring awareness to life first, then lead change without resistance.

✓ The more moments of presence you can show up for, the more *momentum* you are able to build. Momentum is fuel for innovation.

✓ Innovation isn't anything more than a continual streaming of moment-to-moment awareness.

✓ It is very hard to learn new things. It is very hard to live in new patterns. Because it is very hard to let go of what we are convinced we know for sure. As awareness increases, you see the damage that autopilot has had on your people and how it has held them and the organization back from collaboration, innovation, and sustainable growth.

✓ Antithesis of present-moment awareness: Presumption that the folks in the front of the room have all the answers. So your people become passive and move into autopilot, or worse, into resistance.

✓ Your people don't resist change; they resist being changed.

2

Seeing with Fresh Eyes

Emotional connection to your beingness is the stimulus for any change.

When you *feel* possibility, not just understand it intellectually, a transformation occurs within you. That's what happened to the participant's son. When he became aware of his experience, he could then allow himself to move into the next moment, and the next, as he translated the English words into Latin. He was driving his own learning.

He cried with rage before he translated his misery, his brain's last stand on autopilot before the breakthrough. It's the classic form of resistance.

Science of the body says that change occurs chemically in the brain, heart, and gut, but it is the emotional connection that sparks the shift. The three centers get connected together and work as a team for the experience, not just the knowledge.

[**UNLearning needs space and time for the answer to arrive.**]

Emotional connection to your beingness is the stimulus for change. When awareness is guiding possibility where there was little to none just moments before, that's UNLearning. String a whole sequence of those moment-to-moment awarenesses together, and you are building trust.

Out of emotional connection you create trust, and trust generates hope. When you harness those emotional bundles together, you create co-intelligence. As a human being, you are hardwired for it. It's that intelligence in you that wants to connect with other intelligences in favor of the best possible answer, the un-thought-of-option, the most potent solution.

UNLearning needs space and time for the answer to arrive in your body, and then it connects you to other people in the room. Once it does, UNLearning creates a playing field where a whole team, hardwired for connection, moves to collective awareness. The time it takes depends on how hard some hold on to the way it's always been, and how much they resist any sense of being changed.

We've said it before, and it bears repeating, that people don't resist change, they resist being changed.

Are you being a barrier to change by being the one dominating the how, when, where, and who of the change? And if so, how do you think that is affecting the potential for seeing with fresh eyes?

What comes to mind when you think of having fresh eyes?

[*We call it being aware.*]

Have you ever been looking for your keys, become more and more frantic, and in frustration thrown your hands up and exclaimed, "I give up!"? Then you exhaled and felt sorry for yourself for a few moments. Then you circled back to where you looked the first time only to find your keys where you could have sworn you'd already looked?

That's *fresh eyes.*

Fresh eyes occur when you are keeping your awareness supple and soft, like a sponge, available for what you haven't seen or experienced before. It takes being open, curious, and available. Some people think of it as childlike; others call it vulnerable.

We call it being aware.

What these states have in common is that they are outcomes. Each one is a result of presencing.

- Open
- Curious
- Childlike
- Vulnerable

Individually, they build your capacity for awareness. Collectively, they power trust.

It's important to make a distinction here between what popular culture likes to call being present and what we borrow from the Presencing Institute in our work—*presencing*—the act of making moment-to-moment awareness.

GET PRESENT TO THE LEADER YOU HAVEN'T MET … YET

The distinction is both slight, and as wide as the Grand Canyon. When you commit to *being present,* there's an unspoken pressure attached to an underlying fear that you somehow won't be able to do it.

You won't be able to just be.

You won't be able to stop the thoughts, the list-making, the constant chatter in your head about what's next. There's a fear that just being will elude you and you'll be haunted by the thought that you can't do presence. The truth is, being present takes practice. It takes practice to let go of everything you believe that makes you matter. The practice of releasing *how to* in favor of *being* is a doing of sorts. It's the putting-off of having to produce something. The fear of not being able to be continuously in a *state of presence* is a pressure cooker no leader wants to find him/herself in.

This is why so many, most in fact, just don't undertake this work. We believe this simple state is what has led to some of the catastrophic work statistics reported as recently as midyear 2023.

Oak Engage, a UK-based firm researching workplace health, noted that 85% of employees are most motivated when their internal communications are effective. The power of your presence would be able to flip that 85% from disengaged to engaged.

Gallup's Workplace Survey says your engaged employees would be 41% less likely to be absent, and would, as they thrive, miss 53% less work due to health issues. And you would experience an 18% decline in turnover.

You may not want to explore it because inside the idea that you can be present is also the idea that you can *not* be present. It becomes a yin and yang equation. Being present may be optimal, and there will also be times when you are not present and feel you cannot be. The 2023 Predictive Index states that only 22% of companies know what drives their disengagement. Your willingness to be in present-moment awareness could change your business from disengaged to engaged. Let this book be your road map.

Let's say you've created an outline for your life. It's a plan you and your spouse have agreed upon, and now you're "working the plan."

[*Presencing takes practice.*]

You want to succeed in making your plan a reality. Maybe part of it is a map for directions. Places you do and don't want to go. As you pay more attention to the things you don't want, you discover the evidence you need for mounting a case for where you don't want to go. Evidence that reveals the nitty-gritty ways you're not quite good enough to go to those places on your map.

How can that be? The answer usually starts with the dreaded "because." Because your findings support a belief system lodged within you, and it colors every moment of your existence. It stops you from presencing.

Until you start practicing presencing, you will live and work in a perpetual state of a Groundhog Day—same feelings, same thoughts, same outcomes, different day.

In presencing, be prepared to abandon your plan in favor of your longings. Your plan is often so much about how to avoid what you don't want. It becomes nothing more than a layout of everything you worry won't happen. We say that "worry" is a prayer for everything you do not want.

Abandon worrying and replace it with presencing. Yes, it's easier said than done but it's achievable.

Presencing takes practice. It is the act of trusting your observations, thoughts, and feelings. Each one of those observations is attached to a meaning-making structure most think of as part of a belief system, an extrinsic concept, or an intrinsic one.

Think of a chair: the chair has four legs, is made of wood, and has a seat and arms. This is the system of a chair. An extrinsic concept might be: the legs are wobbly, which makes it less of a good chair than one whose legs are sturdy. An intrinsic concept of a chair is that it was carved by your uncle.

Which is the best idea for a chair? At The Institute, we say any time a system connects to a human interaction and emotion, it is more evolved, closer to innovation and more deserving of our trust.

Presencing leads you to what interests you. Being present allows you to connect to the inklings, intuitions, links, or perceptions that surround your interests. Pay attention to those, and the sensations they spark in you. They have important intelligence to impart when you slow down long enough to practice your presencing.

When you're ready to practice presencing, postpone organizing and structuring any ideas too soon. You may have colliding thoughts; thoughts that don't nest neatly or agree. What do these ideas bumping into each other dislodge that's of interest to you? How do you pay attention to them? Often, this is an uncomfortable place, especially for you, dear leader, who is used to deciding what is what.

When you stay present, you slow down the process of deciding. The deciding process may feel like a revving—*openness*. Within it, grasp that your thoughts and images take their endless variety from inside—*curiosity*. You are allowing time for any innate playfulness to have time to be considered—*childlike.* If you are willing, this slowing down will let you move into the heart of your perceptions and of the world around you. This is the core action of the word made popular in corporate life by American professor and writer, Brené Brown—*vulnerability.* What it needs from you is a reconsideration of your mental habits, your belief systems, of how you work.

IF YOU WANT SOMETHING DIFFERENT THAN WHAT YOU'VE GOT

Often, we like to say *everything is valid.* What does that mean? For us, it's this: if it shows up, it deserves to be recognized.

To do that, you're going to have to be aware that whatever *it* is, has shown up. What you do with what shows up is up to you. You now have options, choices, and decisions.

With what you now know about awareness, what happens when you hear yourself saying, "But I had no choice!"

It would be easy to say ... *Snap out of it ... Get over it ... Move on ... Suck it up.* But will that work?

Change has to come from an internal commitment to yourself.

- If you want something different, you're going to have to do something different.

- If you want to do something different, you will have to unlearn whatever belief keeps you driving down the same road.

The good news is that your trust in *present-moment awareness* is the doorway to options and choices.

The decisions you make with options you've gathered is awareness at work. It's you letting go of and moving beyond your Favorite Feelings—your default emotions that run on unchallenged beliefs like, "I'm no good at math." Say it often enough and you live your life with the belief that you'll screw up any math problem. You start avoiding math problems. You make jokes about how bad you are at math. And every time you do, you feel less confident in yourself. But you keep saying it because the belief goes unchallenged, championed by your Favorite Feeling—that little hit that keeps you in your place—a little undeserving. It has become ingrained.

Presencing those default feelings is you recognizing what is occurring in the moment: the present moment awareness that you might not be bad at math after all. Presencing that you want to feel something other than unworthy. Welcome to your glorious, innovative, generous present-moment Self.

[*Awareness has made resisting no longer necessary.*]

For the skeptic who's scanning this page wondering when we're getting to The UNlearning Factor, here's a little data-driven biology.

Science calls present-moment awareness a *direct experience* per *ScienceDirect's* pioneering white paper first revealed in 1981 by Russell H. Fazio and Mark P. Zanna. When the direct experience network in your brain is active, several different brain regions get notified and become even more active. This includes the *insula,* a region that relates to perceiving bodily sensations. The *anterior cingulate cortex* is also activated, which is a region in your brain responsible for switching your attention.

Let's translate that into everyday English: First ... a bodily sensation lets you know something is up. Then awareness bubbles up ... you either switch your attention, or, if you're devoted to your Favorite Feeling, you shoo that pesky sensation away. You may turn on the TV, pick up your smartphone, have a drink, or do some online gambling, just to make sure to drown that nuisance of a feeling.

If, however, you are paying attention, and are willing to be with the sensation, when this direct experience network is activated, you let go, and are no longer thinking intently about the past or future, other people, or yourself. You're not considering much at all.

Rather, you are *experiencing* information coming into your senses in real time.

Awareness is the key that opens the door for you to unlearn. It's not concerned with the past, not even the moment before. Nor is it fixated on the future, not even if that's the moment just about to occur.

It's only once you are aware of what is in this *moment* that you can conceive of being or doing *anything* different.

Once your awareness is in the field—meaning the playing field, the team, the project, the department, the company, your family, your community—it starts to shift through *UNLearning*. When this happens, overcoming your resistance stops being the objective.

Awareness has made resisting no longer necessary.

The reason we started this book with our perspectives on *awareness* is this: when we start making the practice of awareness in the present moment, we can begin to connect to others. When we can connect openly with others, then we move into the space where we look for common purpose. And, when we find commonality, we *collaborate*. Collaborating feels good if those within a team trust each other. They seek more experiences so they can feel that being within the group is where they belong.

And we'll give you this one for free: That feeling they want to feel all the time—that's trust. The more trust you can generate in yourself and others, the greater your engagement.

It's your turn. It's been reported, almost relentlessly, that a significant majority of the workforce is nominally productive … as in 80+%. Using your own burgeoning awareness, what engagement strategy could you create with your team to flip those percentages … even soar to 100% engagement?

GO AHEAD, WE DARE YOU TO INNOVATE FROM YOUR DREAMS— THOSE OH, SO DEEP LONGINGS

- Imagine what you would dream up if you felt you had no restrictions … nothing that could hold you back.

- Imagine what your team could accomplish if full trust was the norm.

- Imagine what you and your team would be to the bottom line … even the world!

Put this book down, take some deep breaths, and close your eyes. Now go ahead and spend some time just imagining … dreaming. And if that's not working, an easy option is to play around with the phrase *what if*.

We human beings are built for dreaming. Allow more time for it. Welcome it. Then share your dreams, which is a supreme act of trust.

Think of a time when you let go of your belief about how it should be and joined the group as you all sought a solution.

Humanity is hurtling through space on a rock being held by gravitational pull of a roiling ball of fusion reactions. So what in the world is keeping you from a little dreaming and collaborating?

Teams, groups, communities are continually moving into a future that is already occurring.

Your having present-moment awareness in those groups is a vital part of having it work for everyone. In a collective state of awareness, and unlearning, your coworkers are no longer functionaries, feeling they are toiling away to make someone else's life better.

Your team members are creating their own best futures. When they are driving change from their awareness, there is no resistance, nothing to overcome, no strain or stress against another will being forced on their knowing. When you are working in this agreement, you are what athletes, artists, inventors often call *the flow* or *the zone*.

Here's the secret sauce you'll want in your pocket as you use *UNLearning*: There is nothing missing in you to stop you from increasing your capacity for presencing. You were born with everything you'll ever need to presence your life and work.

You have everything you will ever need to be a great leader, IF, and only if, you are willing to get present and continue to be present.

Your awareness is the fundamental tool for aligning and engaging yourself with others, and is the doorway to trust and radical, creative energy—to true innovation.

AMP It Up　｜UNLearning Lab

1. What are you doing in your organization to promote moment-to-moment awareness in yourself? In your teams?

2. What's one example you can recall in the recent past where you used your awareness to change a long-held belief in yourself, your team, or about a project?

3. What's one thing you see yourself doing differently when you encounter people or situations where you are experiencing stuckyness?

Key UNLearnings

✓ When you *feel* possibility, not just understand it intellectually, a transformation occurs within you.

✓ When awareness is guiding possibility where there was little or none just moments before, that's *UNLearning.* String a whole sequence of those moment-to-moment awarenesses together, and you are building trust.

✓ Presencing takes practice. It is the act of trusting your observations, thoughts, and feelings. Each one of those observations is attached to a meaning-making structure most think of as part of a belief system, an extrinsic concept, or an intrinsic one.

✓ The good news is that your trust in *present-moment awareness* is the doorway to options and choices.

✓ In a collective state of awareness, and unlearning, your coworkers are no longer functionaries, feeling they are toiling away to make someone else's life better.

3

The Doorway to Trust
through UNLearning

*A full 85% of the workforce, globally, is disengaged
in their work.*

Why do you do the work you do?

*It is awareness that moves your attention and shapes your
intentions. Cultivating present moment awareness with your
Self is the radical source to all creative endeavors. When you
direct your awareness, you will direct energy. When you direct
your energy, you will direct any decision you are making. The
secret sauce that brings it all together is the magic word: trust.*

When we hand our business cards to individuals who
are leaders, they typically feel the card, turn it over,
and then read, *The Institute for UNLearning* out loud.
Looking up, they often ask,

"What is *UNLearning*? What is it all about?"

"What do *you* think it's all about?" we'll ask. They pause,
and smile, and share a time they *unlearned* something. It's
that personal.

UNLearning is the lived experience of unwinding a
point of view, a conceptual bias, in order to arrive at a new

awareness where beliefs, concepts, ideas, and one's how to's can change.

What we notice in our work at The Institute is that people who are invested in presencing, start collaborating for the best possible outcomes. They are collaborating because they have started to trust themselves—what they see and feel—and have started to share that trust with those around them.

[*Sharing creates belonging and belonging engenders trust.*]

Statistics are your wake-up call. In our work, none is more blatant in summing up the cost of running on autopilot, a primary result of being disengaged. Do those who work for you run on autopilot? *Do you?*

Running on autopilot means that you, and those on your team, are going through the motions at work and in life without the benefits of awareness.

At The Institute we call the skill of creating being present, the root of Agile Culture Design™. This skill is really the work of building healthy culture. You thread awarenesses together until they become a belief, then trusting the belief so strongly that you enter collaboration. Internally and externally, trust grows, creating a repeatable cycle that generates ever greater spirals of energy, or *momentum.* When you have collaboration and trust, you are poised for innovation. This energetic dynamic propels a culture to keep designing what it needs to keep making things work. It's agility in action.

This cycle of continuously creating what works best for all is the proving ground of the definition. When you have a culture that keeps working no matter what circumstances it faces, you have Agile Culture. Agile Culture leads to another concept we have developed at The Institute that we call Continuous Renewal Economics. In a brief definition, it's the harnessing of your Agile Culture to bring forward everything that works together for the good of all your business. The mechanics of the people working together becomes the operationalizing of the impact of your goods and services. Sustaining what keeps working best becomes profit. And, from this place, you are building sustainable profitability—an economy.

[*Innovation is just a continual series of moment-to-moment awarenesses.*]

As you flow from one awareness in this moment to another in the next moment, your continual awareness is building what we believe is now and will be the greatest currency of humanity's ability to thrive and evolve—trust.

Continuous renewal is embraced within the process of letting go. The way we define continuous renewal is where you, as a leader, are able to let go of anything that does not serve trust or in anything that does not positively affect collaboration. In the end, you let go of the rigidity that keeps your world manageable, the known: the status quo.

As a leader, you must be aware of this single statistic—the one that led this chapter:

A full 85% of the workforce, globally, is disengaged in their work.

This statistic bears repeating because, sadly, it hasn't budged in more than a decade. As a leader, you must be tuned into the top-line cost: According to Gallup in 2023, employee disengagement costs the world economies 7.8 trillion dollars in lost productivity. In the U.S. alone, half a trillion dollars is blown off annually. What does that mean in salary costs? It translates to $3,400 for every $10,000 an employee is paid. Can you afford to be in this position? We bet not.

[*Blaming them won't change this fact.*]

Today, companies spend more than $100 billion annually trying to improve employee engagement in the workplace. Does it work? We know it doesn't. Based on many of the companies we've worked with, when leaders abdicate real change in favor of box-checking exercises, chances are better than good that the needle on improving engagement isn't going to move much.

As a leader, when you discover your capacity to trust, and model it, you will have taken a giant leap to engaging your teams. When they feel they belong because you trust them, their critical thinking and idea-generating passion for their work comes back online.

Sharing creates belonging, and belonging engenders trust. When your team feels they can contribute and be valued for what they share, they get busy collaborating.

When your people sense you trust them as they witness you trusting yourself, watch them start to share their wildest ideas ... the ones they never felt safe sharing before.

When you stick to rearranging the deck chairs on your personal *Titanic* while you do a dance for your Board of

Directors and shuffle priorities, trust in yourself diminishes exponentially. This leadership style is certainly common for many leaders—the norm for doing business. In fact, it's been normalized to the degree that it has become the expectation.

So ... as a leader, if your employees are representative of 85% of the workforce who are twiddling their thumbs, texting, or who knows what, what are you going to do—starting now—to start reengaging them?

According to The Execu/Search Group, employees agree that managerial support is the most important aspect of company culture, and that 71% would quit if another employer offered even a flexible schedule. Do you know what your employees want? Have you asked?

TAKE A PAGE FROM HISTORY TO FIND YOUR PLACE IN THE FUTURE

Because the debate over how and where to use AI is front and center as we write this book, it's worth using the recent studies to demonstrate how engagement works, and whether AI is going to increase engagement or eradicate it.

AI can change everything in the world except how humans think and behave.

What is AI useful for in the scope of human evolution?

Any creative exploration undertaken without first using Awareness, Mindfulness, and Presence to ground an intention or set of intentions, has a better than average chance of having some kind of cataclysmic rogue impacts on humanity.

Let's go back to Albert Einstein's response to the nascent development of atomic energy. His view was simply, "The unleashed power of the atom has changed everything save our modes of thinking, and we thus drift toward unparalleled catastrophe."

Einstein was clear: Without first understanding what you want as the intention for your discovery, how will you be guided by what you discover?

You cannot set an intention without first becoming deeply aware, mindful, and present.

This book is first and foremost a wake-up call to you as a leader: Begin *right now* to take seriously, more than ever before in your life, the necessity of the *how* and *why* of engaging your teams.

We thought the debate over AI would be a good crux on which to build a case for making a stand for your future, the future of your company, and the planet.

Think about it. What are your intentions for what you think and accomplish in your work and life? What do you envision you are creating for the future of your company?

Let's take Microsoft's new venture with OpenAI for example. What is it for? And what does it do exactly? It defines itself as, "highly autonomous systems that outperform humans *at most economically valuable work.*"

Artificial general intelligence (AGI) refers to AI as "getting to a point where it can figure out a solution to an unfamiliar task." Okay, so we're getting warm now to a future envisioning AI and AGI in it.

Our view at The Institute is that OpenAI is good at taking over tasks that, until recently, have been the domain of humans. So far, it's fairly widely accepted that spelling and grammar AI is a good thing. And figuring out the fewest moves for maximum efficiency on a production line is just good business. But this is not the focus here.

What *is* at the heart of this conversation is that as a society we have dumbed-down our capabilities by micro-managing the hell out of what we see as productivity in our companies—from the top down.

When The Institute starts working with a company, we often discover entire departments working at skill and competency levels at least one to two levels below their capabilities. So, rather than attending to work that demands critical thinking, many are working from sheets of rules, regulations, and protocols that demand strict adherence.

How connected can you be if all you are doing is following the letter of the law?

This disengagement of the workforce (85% globally) has happened slowly over decades since the Industrial Revolution. The internal logic sounds like: What can a machine do faster, more accurately, more repetitively and repeatably than a human? Will it generate more profit? Will it generate more security for the one(s) in charge? If yes, then go for it! Will AI put people out of work? Yes, but this is just business, and we have to make decisions based on what's best for the company.

What seems to be left out of the equation as AI replaces humans in accomplishing tasks and entire jobs is this: When a machine does what you were doing until yesterday, *what does that free you up to take on today?*

If AI has not impacted your company yet, no doubt it will in some capacity in the near future. Your employees will first need a mind shift into the space where they can be supported while they learn a whole new set of skills.

Again, and just our opinion, AI without commensurate Emotional Intelligence (EQ) is just another money grab.

To balance AI and EQ, you'll have to work on your Awareness, Mindfulness, and Presence, which are the hardcore skills that make up a healthy EQ. Otherwise, you're part of the money-grab with a lot of mea culpas spoken in hushed solemnity from whatever mountaintop the issuers have ensconced themselves, in the wake of whatever destruction du jour the race for more produces.

And the power of your EQ and its impact is what this book is all about.

It's important to note the scope of AI's influence. CNBC reported as late as April 8, 2023, that Microsoft has invested upwards of $13 billion in its partnership with OpenAI. And the startup's valuation has hit roughly $29 billion. That's a tidy 50% net return on one of the hottest names in artificial intelligence.

Warren Buffet, Chairman of the Board at Berkshire Hathaway, was recently introduced to OpenAI and told Microsoft founder Bill Gates:

> It's very interesting. It can translate the Constitution into Spanish in one second. But the computer could not tell jokes .... Bring it back when I can ask it, "How are you going to get rid of the human race?" I want to see what it says and pull the plug [out] before it does it.

The New York Times, May 30, 2023, published a signed statement from three hundred and fifty artificial intelligence industry leaders. The article reads:

> [They are] planning to warn the world that artificial intelligence technology they are building may pose

an existential threat to humanity and should be
considered a societal risk on par with pandemics
and nuclear wars.

The leaders' one-sentence statement: "Mitigating the risk
of extinction from AI should be a global priority alongside
the other societal-scale risks, such as pandemics and nuclear
war."

Chief among those leaders, Sam Altman, chief executive
of OpenAI; Demis Hassabis, chief executive of Google
DeepMind; and Dario Amodei, chief executive of Anthropic.

In the face of the next Cyber Gold Rush, will this
statement be heard? Or will it be trampled under the
stampede to extract as much as possible out of AI before it's
too late? Where will you land, dear leader?

If history is any indicator ....

We bring this conversation into the mix and at the same
time we are asking you how you will lead in the 21st century
and beyond?

While AI may be supercool and drool-worthy, without
empathy, emotional intelligence, and a deep interest in the
well-being of others, it is motivated by the self-interest of a
few folks who know how to claim a grab-worthy investment.

Did we have to make an atomic bomb out of atomic
technology? Nope. But we did.

The first thing Oppenheimer created out of his genius:
music from the quantum energy of molecules.

In case you think we're just musing, we are not. For
starters we could have gone directly from atomic energy to
clean energy. The U.S. Office of Nuclear Energy published
alternative uses for atomic energy in March of 2022.

- Commercial reactors can be used to power desalination plants.

- Provide heat for metal refining.

- Generate hydrogen as a clean burning alternative fuel for vehicles.

History's capacity to repeat itself is speeding up. Fast-forward fifty years from the invention of the atomic bomb to 1997 when the young engineers of Six Degrees began inventing what we now know as Social Media. These moguls have since made personal fortunes in the billions from their nifty inventions. That's about six white guys and anyone in their sphere of influence.

We will not be fully aware for decades to come of the devastating consequences Social Media has had and continues to have on our evolution as a species.

The film *The Social Dilemma,* released in 2020, had shocking statistics and interviews with some of these inventors. They speak as if they never thought beyond its being *cool,* and while they never say it out loud in the film, oh *so* lucrative.

These same gurus now admit that they do not use nor permit their children to use Social Media platforms. What have they discovered that they want to protect their offspring from? Could it be that the impact of Social Media usage is disconnection from human interaction? A growing encroachment of the illusion of connection is in reality an epidemic of loneliness and isolation. The inventors have washed their hands and absolved themselves of any wrong-doing because they never intended some of the dire consequences our global society now faces.

What did they intend? What did they do at the outset to set clear intentions?

Meanwhile, teen suicide is up in alarming rates, and we are lonelier as a society than ever before. We have lost our ability to value the spirit of community, indeed the whole virtue of esprit de corps, which literally means the spirit of the body. When translated into colloquial usage from the Oxford dictionary: *a feeling of pride, fellowship, and common loyalty shared by the members of a particular group.*

One has to wonder.

The didactic debate over artificial intelligence is somehow a perfect symbol of its place in our imaginations at this moment in history. It is something that will eliminate countless jobs, boost creativity, and put an end to drudgery. Or perhaps it's a monstrous force that will take over our planet and enslave or eliminate humanity.

According to a new survey commissioned by Microsoft, it released its 2023 "New Future of Work Report" with 31,000 responses. Many see AI as both a benefit and a threat:

- 49% of employees are scared of losing their jobs to AI.
- 70% hope that AI will help them manage increasing workloads.

While it's already eliminating jobs, it's also likely that AI will be taking over even more menial tasks, so human beings can move on to much more collaborative work.

That is, *if* they are willing to learn new ways of being, thinking, and doing. If you are willing to lead by first UNLearning, this is the single most important reason that we discuss Awareness, Mindfulness, and Presence throughout this book.

If you're an employer, consider how your business might use AI and how it may affect it. You also need to give employees some clear guidance on how AI might affect them in the near- and mid-term. Give employees a voice on how they can be part of building more meaningful work for themselves and in turn drive your business success.

As Microsoft notes, more employers seem interested in helping employees with AI than replacing them with AI. On the other hand, roughly one out of every six employers is hoping AI will allow them to operate with fewer people.

Microsoft's survey makes a case for three aspects for your business's well-being amid the growth of AI:

AI works for employees.

- Administrative work (76%)
- Analysis (79%)
- Creative work (73%)

AI works for employers.

- Increasing employee productivity (31%)
- Helping employees with necessary but repetitive and/or mundane tasks (29%)
- Increasing employee well-being (26%)
- Reducing headcount (16%)

IBM's chief executive, Arvind Krishna, told *Bloomberg News* on May 1, 2023, "I could easily see 30% of the company's back-office roles replaced by AI over the next five years."

What no one is asking Arvind is, what is he doing to engage that 30% in inventing a future where they collaborate in more meaningful work?

AI puts companies under a microscope: attend to your productivity issues.

- Not enough uninterrupted time to focus during the workday (68%)
- Drowning in email and communication (68%)
- Ineffectual meeting overload is cutting into productivity (72%)

Our UNLearning Factor is a great place to start making real change in productivity, and it can happen as early as your next meeting.

AI can point to a new mindset for work altogether.
- Employees need new skills—primarily soft skills (82%)
- Analytical judgment (30%)
- Flexibility (29%)
- Emotional Intelligence (27%)

Leaders who have opted not to engage The Institute for the development of their teams have most often deemed our work to be too mired in *soft skills* to be useful. And, lest we begin to sound like a broken record, The UNLearning Factor is a juggernaut for engaging all four of the soft skills the Microsoft Study examines.

Why bring atomic energy and the advent of AI into the dialogue? We want to paint a picture of what occurs when leaders do not take seriously the importance of setting intention in building business. And, we want to demonstrate the collateral damage to the reality of human connection when intentions are left undefined.

DO YOU HAVE WHAT IT TAKES TO LEAD IN THE 21st CENTURY?

It's time for us to ask the question that will either stir you to reconsider what you're doing now or leave this book in a drawer.

> What would be the value in reimagining how you get work done in your company?
> And perhaps more important, why do you do the work you do?

There is light at the end of the tunnel: When companies seek out higher levels of employee engagement, they experience in excess of a 21% increase in profits, according to Oak Engage. Does this interest you? We hope so.

With these data, it appears that investing in employee engagement would be a prudent move for a significant payoff for you and your employees. Of course, you'd first have to become aware that whatever you're now doing as a leader may not be compelling. The result: Your workforce is not engaged. There's that pesky fact again.

The act of participating in the process of presencing we explained in Chapter One is the very core of trust. It is the bedrock of how you trust yourself, and then, how you trust the thoughts, feelings, and actions of others.

HOW YOU APPROACH TRUST WILL MAKE YOU ... OR BREAK YOU

At the start of this chapter, we said that trust would be the most important currency of humanity's future. This is where the rubber meets the road. We will not evolve as a species without it.

[*A brittle crust forms over the idea.*]

Here's the good news. Alternatives to what you have now are already and always arriving ... *if* you're willing to practice presencing. When you do, you are always in the discovery mode.

There's a fallacy alive in corporate cultures today and it may be alive in your own. It's the belief that as the leader, your plan brings something new to the entire system by your mere existence. Because you are the leader, your plan naturally must be the best plan. Wrong.

As the leader, are you receptive to revision and refinement of your plan? Whatever is needed to make it better ... or great or innovative? If your answer is no, the practice of presencing is for you.

A warning here is necessary. When an idea is created, there is typically the urge to grasp immediately onto it and hurl it against the cosmic corporate wall to see what sticks. What sticks is what so often is used to make a plan ... when it may not be the best stuff.

So how do you know when it is the best stuff?

Don't you get a feeling, a gut reaction, a confirmation? What do you trust in those moments? Wouldn't it be a marvelous thing for you and your teams to have such robust inner knowing from practicing presencing, that you could bank it (literally)? That is trust at work.

This spot can be an extremely uncomfortable place for many to be in. We call it the space between the no longer and the not yet. Cultivating a resilience to being in this zone, this I-don't-know space, is a critical part of learning presencing. Trust cannot happen without it.

Without trust, there is a belief that all must be put in order as soon as possible, and that you, the leader, had better get it handled. This is a useless distraction, and one that creates a false sense of priority for teams. The first thing everyone does is haul him/herself onto the bandwagon of priorities.

Any naysayers are kicked off the team, and presencing goes out the window. A brittle crust forms over the idea. Predictable results ensue.

If you can continue with the practice of presencing, you will keep your engagement high and innovation inclusive. It's the secret sauce that our UNLearning Factor delivers. It takes a tremendous amount of courage to trust in yourself, in your people, and in the time it takes for trust to grow.

We worked with a team leader in the Armed Forces whose outlook could have been classified as bitter. When we began our discovery with him, he didn't trust the process he was part of. Or rather, he trusted it to work against him and his entire team. This bitter man led a group of thirty engineers.

When we interviewed him, his answers came through slathered in a veneer of contempt for the system that subjugated him and thwarted his good intentions at every turn. He was convinced that he would never reach his goals. Essentially, he had given up on them and, as a result, he'd given up on his team, and, perhaps most tragic, himself.

What we learned in our executive coaching sessions was that he had recently experienced a failed personal relationship of half-truths, lies, and betrayal. It became painfully obvious that this experience was so traumatic it had colored every part of this man's life.

We went to work. It was during the height of the pandemic, and we made sure the team built in time to be seen and heard by one another. All sessions started with our foundational modules: Focus, Questions, the DISC Assessment, and Context. We invigorated the team's ability to communicate effectively with one another.

[*Trust. It is now and will be the single greatest currency of the coming generation.*]

It didn't take long before team members were injecting humor into their meetings. We taught them how to have powerful and effective meetings—the essence of this book. Meetings took on a tone of *collaboration*. The old habit of grousing for an hour about how the system was broken, worked against them, and taking turns nitpicking all the wrongs of leadership were axed ... not by us, by them!

Something altogether magical happened to the leader through the process. His bitterness began to ebb. He began to trust himself again. He reignited his relationship with his team and built it by leading with trust. He began assuming positive intent with each of them and expected the best from his team. And guess what? They started delivering it.

The leader wanted to do more for them. For the first time in his career, he began having reviews and regular one-on-one meetings with his team leaders. As he trusted the process of building relationships, his trust increased for himself and for others. As it increased, his love for his work and for the people he was leading also grew. He not only started making decisions to move his projects forward, but he also began collaborating with his team on new projects and took the initiative to develop and implement them.

Trust. It is now and will be the single greatest currency of the coming generation.

At The Institute, we like to think of engaging trust as *assuming positive intent.* And, to keep yourself in a state of awareness, you must first be ready to accept that off and on, every day for the rest of your life, you're going to have feelings that want your attention, and that make you extremely uncomfortable.

[*It's like living a double life.*]

Take that present moment, give the feeling your attention, stay with the discomfort, and get curious about what it wants of you. Knowing *that* is awareness. Staying with the discomfort is trust.

WORKING AGAINST TRUST ... THE COSTLIEST DECEPTION

Present-moment awareness cannot surface if you are busy covering up, stuffing down, or trying in some way to *rid yourself* of an emotion you think you don't have time to deal with: the one that is keeping you from success; the one that is keeping you from accomplishment; the one that is stealing from your bottom line, or the one that haunts you.

You get used to reaching for the activities that hold those powerful emotions at bay. Those activities are avoidance techniques, ones that take up enormous amounts of energy and mental bandwidth. They're also designed to prevent you from getting into a close relationship with and trusting your emotional life.

Scientific American reported in its December 2018 article, "The Brain's Autopilot Mechanism Steers Consciousness," that the unconscious mind has shown the brain makes judgments and decisions quickly and automatically. That means that you continuously make predictions about future events, often unconsciously, as they are happening. Without new information, your brain will continue to predict along the same neural pathways it has set up.

It's like living a double life. Your true and authentic self is suffocated out of having a say about how you can move toward what you most long for. In this state, you're living outside the realm of your present-moment awareness. Without your present-moment awareness, your presencing, your trust is almost impossible.

At The Institute, we call this state, *living with your Favorite Feelings.* Favorite Feelings, which we mentioned in the previous chapter, give you a false sense of safety—a better the devil you know—kind of half-life, where there is no space in your consciousness for new awareness to show up.

It's the ultimate stuckyness place—the constant reach for the same go-to behaviors and beliefs, while fully expecting a different outcome because you're working so hard for it.

Even though it keeps proving to you that it isn't working.
Even though it's eroding your capacity to trust.

The biggest issue keeping CEOs up at night today is the same as it has been for a decade: They can't get their workforce to innovate. At the Global Leadership Summit just before COVID-19 reared its head, it was the #1 issue for attendees. Yet fewer than three out of ten had any strategy in place to engage their workers.

Could that be you?

[*Everyone, and we mean everyone, deserves to be cared for.*]

We suspect ... no, we know ... that your employees want to be on board. They want to make a valuable contribution to your vision and your company.

What seems to have slipped through the cracks in leadership awareness is that to do that, people need to know they have been seen and heard. They need to know they belong to something meaningful, so they know how to focus their contributions. In short: Everyone, and we mean everyone, deserves to be cared for.

BRINGING YOUR CORE BACK TO LIFE

When we work with a team, we spend a good deal of time bringing participants into *awareness of their core belief systems.* Beliefs that keep them bound to working harder at what keeps proving it isn't working. One of the most telling results of tuning out is the years of diminishing returns that result. When leaders don't tune in, and choose to drop out, the result is chronic disengagement. When your workforce is not engaged, your business will take the hit. Blaming them won't change this fact.

INTEGRATING INTELLECT AND EMOTION PUTS YOU IN THE FIELD OF TRUST

We recently worked with a group of nine men who'd been working together for over two decades. Each was interviewed separately to get a sense of what he thought of his work, the environment, his leader, what he still hoped to achieve, and where his real pain was.

[*Oh, the astrologers are here!*]

What we heard as we listened were words found directly under the surface that described the disappointment, fear, and hurt each had been carrying. We asked each person what he wanted, and how he imagined the world, the one he longed for, and the one he longed for his children and grandchildren.

Each question was designed to give the man across from us permission to become aware of a dream that he'd forgotten.

One of the men, Darin, scoffed at us when we came into his office. "Oh, the astrologers are here!" He rolled his eyes for emphasis. An hour later, he was laughing and even shed some tears as he shared the truth about what he dreamed he wanted to achieve but had given up hope of ever having.

Others on the team called him Eeyore. *He's just so negative* seemed to be the consensus.

Even after his breakthrough in his office, Darin came to the first day's group session determined to prove we were consultant phonies. That we were not going to break him. In his defense, the team had undergone a two-year stint with a consultancy who had cost the division a small fortune with no results. Darin was going to send us home, defeated. He was committed to it because the cost of owning his part in working on autopilot for a couple of decades was too costly to admit ... to himself ... to others.

What we witnessed over the course of the next few days was nothing short of transformational.

On the second day, Darin transitioned from Eeyore to participant, and he began opening up and offering answers in the room. By the third day, he was smiling and joking. He acknowledged how his attitude had contributed to the team's being stuck. He suggested brilliant solutions to issues the team had faced for years.

The other team members shared their experiences, connecting through acknowledging similar emotions, and that's when the shift took over the group and Darin turned into a Tigger ... no longer Eeyore to his teammates.

Rather than meeting to share their resistance, cynicism, and masking their disillusionment, the team shared what was working; what they loved about the work they were doing; what successes they were having; and how they could find solutions to their challenges.

They were using the energy from their awareness, collaboration, and the feeling of shared experience. And, by acknowledging the things that were working, the team found a renewed sense of what they could accomplish. Now they could work together to find solutions to challenging issues they'd faced for years. For the first time, in some cases, they began moving toward belonging again.

The spirit of releasing and letting go of the way they had always done it took over. They were playful with one another.

Their awareness of one another shifted. They no longer saw themselves as defeated, and browbeaten by a system that seemed to be working against their success. Then ...

- Their awareness opened them to options.

- They realized they could make different choices and share their emotions. They could feel the positive collective energy from the group, and the collaborative intelligence they were generating.

- The team was ever so ready to trade in the way it had been. They made agreements and committed to what they most wanted.

Two things were at work: The way they had felt about how it had been; and the way they wanted to feel going forward.

What did we do?

- We asked them questions about what they wanted, how they felt now, and how they wanted to feel.

- We asked them where they could see themselves employing their new awarenesses.

- We asked them how they wanted to feel at the end of each workday.

- We asked them what they wanted to be accountable for and why.

- We asked them how they wanted to be remembered, and for what.

They didn't connect first on the most brilliant idea. Rather they connected through how they felt. And to do that, they first had to become *aware* of how they felt. They UNLearned together in those few days. Their cynicism—which was tanking their leadership—was nothing more than a cover-up for the pain they had experienced at being separated from what they most desired.

Once they reconnected with awareness and shared it, a new bond was forged. They trusted one another.

They'd reconnected by being available to what they wanted more than what they had, and dare we say, vulnerable to how they felt and what they wanted.

When the third day concluded, the division director said,

> I've never seen Darin so active and positive. I'd forgotten how brilliant a thinker he is. I want us to continue this momentum. Can you come back and work with all of our managers?

Our reply was, "We'll do you one better. We'll make sure everyone in your organization is creating ongoing momentum *for themselves.*"

When your team starts to really listen and hear each other's answers, team members start vibrating at a higher frequency. This is *cellular awareness.* They become vulnerable to one another's needs and desires. That's when trust begins to have a real impact. Trust is the energy that keeps on giving—think of the Energizer Bunny.

That's what trust delivers: a verve for collaboration that keeps on going and going and going—minus the floppy pink ears.

We know from The Muse, companies experience 43% higher engagement when employees receive feedback at least once a week. A decrease in management feedback results in a lower engagement by 18%. Connecting with your employees in meaningful feedback counts.

UNLearning through your awareness takes you into transparent communication. You no longer need to mask or hide your wild ideas, or the emotions that accompany them. When you are transparent, you are in the act of trusting. The more often and deeper you trust yourself, the more willing you are to trust others. And that feeling will move you, along with your team, toward collaboration and innovation.

In short, we challenge you to trust your feelings. You've spent a career pouring over spreadsheets and assembling strategies from a million data points distilled to make a case for achieving an outcome. What if you could move from achieving to accomplishing?

We're inviting you to shed your own failure of nerve and, rather than look for one more data set to back your gut, go to your people and cultivate some real-live-energy trust.

You and your team need to understand the difference between achievement and accomplishment. Achievement doesn't need trust to happen. Accomplishment cannot happen without it.

You go from succeeding at any cost on your own, to collaborating for success with others. In fact, you cannot imagine doing it without the whole team. A culture begins to emerge. A culture that can innovate anything.

AMP It Up | UNLearning Lab

Here are questions you will want to ask as a leader if you
have a "Darin" on your team.

1. What is it that "Darin" believes he has to protect?

2. What's doesn't he trust about his own feelings?

3. What needs to shift in him so he is able to re-engage?

Key UNLearnings

✓ A full 85% of the workforce, globally, is disengaged
in their work.

✓ UNLearning is the lived experience of unwinding a
point of view, or a conceptual bias, in order to arrive
at a new awareness where beliefs, concepts, ideas,
and their how-to's can change.

✓ Integrating intellect and emotion puts you in the
field of trust.

✓ Agile Culture Design is the skill to thread awarenesses
together until they become a belief, then trusting the
belief so strongly you enter collaboration.

✓ Sharing creates belonging and belonging engenders
trust.

SECTION II
THE UNLEARNING FACTOR BLUEPRINT

This section covers the five-step process in The UNLearning Factor. Each chapter gives you the step-by-step format to build engagement back into your teams while reducing the stress and effort commonly associated with any kind of systemic change. In these blueprint chapters, we've included the benefits you and your teams can expect to receive when you implement these simple steps into the fabric of your daily interactions.

4

The UNLearning Factor
Your Five-Step Process
and Ultimate Guide to Leading
Change Without Resistance

Welcome to The UNLearning Factor, five steps that will
lead to change without resistance *... steps that will*
help your team succeed and soar.

Every interaction we have at The Institute for UNLearning continues reinforcing our belief that each and every one of us is where we are today as a result of the decisions we've made so far. So here you are ... with everyone else.

In this moment, you have the opportunity to create **change for your organization without resistance**. Your employees are not resisting and you are not resisting.

Awareness. Mindfulness. Presence (AMP).

There are things you have a choice about. When you stand in the presence of this moment, you have the chance to access something outside the collection of decisions and choices you've made up until now. So much depends upon where you put your attention: *where you focus*.

Your mind now has a primary role. It is to keep moving toward what it is focused on. You have a choice to reclaim your personal power. It starts by acknowledging and owning what you are focused on. It is neither right nor wrong, good nor bad, more nor less. It is just what is happening in this moment.

This realization impacted us deeply: If your mind is already designed to keep you moving toward what you focus on, *how do you use that?*

The key question that comes to mind is, *what do I want?*

You may have experienced an interaction that left you saying, "That really frustrated me!" When you release the focus on your reaction to the event, the bottom line is that something happened. The choice you made in your reaction was to be *frustrated* by what happened.

That decision doesn't make you wrong, or bad, or less than. But it can leave you feeling at a loss or stuck. And that feeling can have you driving to double down about how right you are and how wrong the other person or group is. That's when the resistance begins.

Human beings are meaning makers. We can't help it. When we see a gap in understanding we run to fill it. And we do all this meaning-making in relationships too.

In the end, and in the beginning, it comes down to your relationships and the quality of them. The more you are willing to understand yourself, the more you can take the time to understand others and where they are coming from.

The next few pages are going to challenge you in some way: your beliefs, your processes, the systems you've put into play that make your world go 'round. What do you believe you're ready to UNLearn?

[*When in doubt, instead of telling, ask.*]

The key point here: You have a choice in the moment before your decision to be frustrated. Your choice, your decision, directly impacts how things will go from that point forward.

There are five steps to making this paradigm shift for yourself as a leader, for your teams, their teams, and their teams' teams. It works with personal relationships—your spouse, siblings, parents, and children. It's regenerative, evolutionary communication or what we call Continuous Renewal Economics that was mentioned in the previous chapter.

Step One

Start by asking. When in doubt, instead of telling, ask. If you're feeling unsure about what's next, ask. When you feel the room isn't with you, ask. When you feel the room is really with you, ask.

[*Stay curious.*]

Start your next meeting by relieving yourself of being the smartest one in the room tasked with having all the answers. Ask ...

What's working now?
Are you getting the results you want and need?

Step Two

Resist moving into the "go mode." Stay present in the question. Be the great explorer. Do it with enormous curiosity and the verve to learn from others.

Ask ...

> *What is contributing most to what is being done that's causing it to work?*
> *When and where is it happening?*

What's going to be different in a meeting that starts by acknowledging people for what they have done right and how they did it vs what they did wrong?

What's going to be different in the level of openness and cooperation?

How will your questions affect the sense of team cooperation and level of trust?

Explore all that can be learned from understanding what is causing what's working to *actually work*. Give people time to express the sinews and tendons of the *WHY* it's working. Let them hear their own answers.

Step Three

Clarify the goal, the outcome, and potential results you want to produce.

There are two key factors that influence the impact of continuing to be in exploration mode during this important step.

First, what is your sense of the benefits of having had the exploration of the first two steps before beginning the clarity of the desired objective?

Second, and maybe even more significant, is the importance of freedom from the far too familiar practice of you, the leader, stating the goal; then following up by asking something like, "Everybody clear on what we're doing?"

Go around the room (yes, it will take longer) and have each team member share his/her understanding of the goals and objectives. What do you see as the most important benefits of this approach?

Think of it as the pay now or pay later plan.

The first three steps clarify where you really want and need to put your attention. Getting from where you are to where you want to be is the goal, not getting mired in problem-solving before you know what the road map forward looks like.

Asking a question like, **what do we need to know about what didn't work to help us get to our goal?** This is far more strategic than asking, *what didn't work?* And *why didn't it work?* Or *who's fault is it?* At this point in the process, a common tendency is to want to get right to the action.

There is a vital step in between; another key to the "pay now or pay later plan."

Step Four

What will be the benefit(s) when you achieve the goals and meet the objectives you've explored?

Again, this is NOT the place for you to tell your people what the benefits will be. Your work will be in resisting your foresight, instincts, and experience and just ASK them

[*It's time for the action.*]

When you get good at shutting up and listening after asking the critical Step Four question, you may want to do the mental version of a conga line and explore these sorts of follow-up questions:

> *Who will benefit most?*
> *What will be the benefit for the customers?*

At this stage in the process, you may also want to ask:

> *What will be the cost if we don't achieve our goal?*

This is especially true when there is significant impact to people for not reaching the objective.

Either way, how your people apply themselves to what they are doing has a direct impact on their understanding of *why* they're doing it. It is the classic WIIFM—what's-in-it-for-me scenario.

You have now tilled, fertilized and seeded the ground for it to produce. It's time for the action.

Step Five

You, dear leader, *must remain the explorer here.* Stay curious. You're probably brimming with ideas, solutions, fixes, experiences, stories and how-to's. Find a way to shelve them for later. You may need them. You may never need them. What you want to do here is *listen.* Deeply. For what's being said and what's not quite being said ... yet. Here's your kickoff question:

> *What can we be doing more of, less of, better or differently to get closer to the desired goal/outcome/objective?*

Consider the mental process this approach activates from the beginning.

Assuming that buy-in is important, notice how it starts back in Step One.

It is easier to get your people to buy-in from the perspective of what they are doing well, doing better, and doing right, than it ever will be if you ask them to admit that what they've been doing is wrong, falls short, didn't meet the mark, or failed.

Everything from Step Two through Step Five is about deepening and directing the buy-in that's already been achieved in Step One.

Now loop back to Step One through Step Five and integrate them into your organization as the new norm.

Welcome to the pioneering and transformational five-step process of The UNLearning Factor. We go deeper into each step in the upcoming chapters to help guide you to your own excellence as a leader and show you how to lead without resistance. Steps that will see your team soaring with success and you as well.

AMP It Up | UNLearning Lab

1. What position do you take now that avoids facing the pay now, pay later plan?

2. What are you doing now that is a rehash of what you've always done to support the diminishing benefits of incremental improvement?

3. What are the ways you are truly operating strategically?

4. How do you know when your teams are truly engaged?

Key UNLearnings

✓ If your mind is already designed to keep you moving toward what you focus on, *how do you use that?*

✓ Human beings are meaning makers. We can't help it. When we see a gap in understanding, we run to fill it. And we do all this meaning-making in relationships too.

✓ Step One: Start by asking. When in doubt, instead of telling, ask. If you're feeling unsure about what's next, ask. When you feel the room isn't with you, ask.

✓ Step Two: Resist moving into the "go mode" and stay present in the question. Be the great explorer. Do it with enormous curiosity and the verve to learn from others.

✓ Step Three: Clarify the goal, the outcome, and potential results you want to produce.

✓ Step Four: What will be the benefit(s) when you achieve the goals and meet the objectives you've explored?

✓ Step Five: What you want to do here is *listen*. Deeply. For what's being said and what's not quite being said.

✓ It is easier to get your people to buy-in from the perspective of what they are doing well, doing better, and doing right, than it ever will when you ask them to admit that what they've been doing is wrong, falls short, didn't meet the mark, or failed.

5

STEP ONE: Take the Plunge

Can There Be Change without Resistance?
In one word ... YES!

Nowhere is it more important to reclaim your awareness than in waking up to the truth about how you have been conned and conditioned throughout your business life. If you've been directed to implement change and improvements from a source narrowly focused on seeking out problems and fixing them, you've been bamboozled. And, whether you register it or not, your truthiness notices the bamboozling.

When your truth barometer notices the gap between what is truth and what is not, in swoops the resistance you wanted to avoid in the first place. The resistance you feel, that's you protecting yourself from being bamboozled again ... and again. But because you've been conditioned NOT to pay attention to the flag-waving truthiness, you agree somewhere inside yourself to live with that constant little jiggly feeling by resisting it.

Instead, you go after fixing problems believing that will relieve the resistance in you. But it doesn't; it persists like heartburn. That resistance is the biggest obstacle to producing the results you want and need most.

That resistance is called *problem-solving*. It lives in direct opposition to creating from the authentic truth you possess about the how and why of a thing. Nothing will generate resistance quicker and more effectively.

Now, think about it from your own experience:

> How long did it take for the resistance to show up when you introduced a change? The typical response we get from asking that question is: Immediately!

It's time to ask:

> What would be the benefits of being able to accomplish quickly the improvements you most require? And what would be the value of being able to make these improvements without the stress and effort normally associated with change?

Before revealing the *how to* of achieving change without resistance, it's time to quash outdated thoughts about change that are ripe for UNLearning ....

- It is human nature to resist change. Not true. It is a learned behavior.

- If there is a change, there will be resistance that needs to be overcome. Not true. If you didn't cause the resistance, you wouldn't have to work so hard to overcome it.

- Change is hard. Not true. You learned to do it in a way that causes it to be hard!

- People resist change. Not true. They resist being changed.

There is an alternative, the *how-to* for implementing *changes without the typical resistance.*

The first thing to consider is an initiative of yours that has eluded your best efforts so far. You have not been successful in achieving the results you desire. It was one where you tried everything you've learned to do; everything you were told to do; and you were unable to achieve your desired results.

It starts with STEP ONE.

[*Contrary to popular business beliefs, problem-solving has become one of the major obstacles to business success.*]

At The Institute for UNLearning, with more than thirty years of facilitating, we've seen that The UNLearning Factor for Mastery-Based Leadership works every time, and in every situation we encounter, well, except for two. There have been two instances where we bowed out from an engagement. In each case, the leader insisted that he was the one who had it all figured out already. More on that later.

When we refer to mastery-based leadership, we are talking about shared outcomes that work for the employees, the company, its partners, and clients.

Let's be sure you are clear about what we are saying here when we refer to shared outcomes. We mean that everyone who touches or is touched by that outcome is better for it. They are the outcomes from deep collaboration and calculated risk in the service of innovation. They leave with a sense of accomplishment.

It's a little thing we picked up along the way that's become the core of our work. It's about how everyone deserves to be cared for. And likely, you're where you are because someone or many someones cared about your well-being and success.

If you're kicking back saying, "Nope, I did this all on my own," this book probably isn't for you. Why? Because the bare-naked truth is you didn't do any of it alone. And, because the idea of caring is worth your career.

THE GRAVE MISUNDERSTANDING BETWEEN INSPIRATION AND MOTIVATION

Leaders who believe they are responsible for motivating their people have missed the boat, literally. If you are navigating your company's success and guiding your teams by inspiring them, you're going to find they'll do all their own motivating. It's the inverse of the saying attributed to Captain Bligh, of the ship *Bounty,* "The beatings will continue until morale improves."

So often, motivation is a disguise for getting what you want by shaming your employees through your version of "you're not doing enough, but here's how you can meet my standards."

Take the 2022 Gartner Research Study on improving salespeople's motivation, for example: the headline shouted out and teased: *Increase Sellers' Motivation, Hunger and Energy to Close More Deals.* It got our attention.

> Was it possible?
>
> Or was it just another headline thrown out to draw in those who are doing business at any price?
>
> Was there something Gartner had uncovered that the rest of us didn't know?

We were already starting to hyperventilate with the possible revelation that there was something to be uncovered that would change the way we look at human potential. And then, we stopped and reread the title. *Increase Sellers' Motivation, Hunger and Energy to Close More Deals.*

First off, the title is a directive. It's telling you what to want, and supposing the study's authors have the answers. Sure, they got data points by surveying salespeople, and then they sharpened the data to a fine poker and proceeded to wax expertly about how to wield motivation, hunger, and energy. For what outcome, we queried? Was it for the well-being of salespeople? Maybe.

How it read to us: *Want to close more deals? Get your people motivated, hungry, and with focused energy for your ultimate gain.* And then it's wrapped up in a vague bumper sticker ... *during these uncertain selling times.* That's the catch-all for, *"we don't have a clue what's really going on."*

"Uncertain selling times" was the blame for anything going poorly in a sales team's environment. Statements like *"fluctuating stakeholders on the buyer's side,"* and *"unclear buyer process,"* and that old chestnut, *"misaligned customer needs,"* also floated to the top of the manure heap.

Being uncertain was the most truthful piece of the entire study. At The Institute, we believe wholeheartedly in not having a clue, in being squarely in the I-don't-know space. And what you do when you're in that space is what makes all the difference between more of the same results doing it the way you're doing it, or something completely different. Your choice.

It is always your choice.

The Gartner directive may sound like music to your ears, a three-pronged approach to haul you out of that quagmire of uncertainty, but what Gartner doesn't address in their research is the underlying, unwitnessed lack of care for protecting, advancing, and promoting what creates the motivation, energy, and hunger in a human being.

What Gartner does, as so many do, is take the idea of stress and burnout as a matter of fact in doing business. In 2022, the Virtira Study revealed that 49% of remote employees are exhausted after daily virtual meetings. The Oak Engage group reports that only 29% are satisfied with their opportunities for advancement, one of the primary causes of stress and burnout in the workplace.

Gartner's fix for the problem would be worthy if, as a nation of workers, we weren't suffering from burnout, depression, anger, despair, sadness, anxiety, and the host of ailments associated with all of these.

Kudos to companies who recognize that stress is a factor in the workplace. For employees, the norm is that it is their responsibility to manage their own stress even though it is created by the workplace itself, and the leaders who run it.

Is stress all bad?

No. Science shows that a measure of stress is actually a catalyst for creative work as noted by Kelly McGonigal, author of *The Upside of Stress*. But there is a BIG IF to it. If stress is allowed, even encouraged to compound, not just for a day, but a month, a year or years, it will consume employees.

How aware are you of the level of your people's pain and stress as a result of working harder and harder to get results like *"hungry, energy, and motivated"*?

We asked ourselves, was there a big secret answer to these complexities? Gartner's revelations rolled out:

> *More motivation for your Sales Teams.* That's right. Incentivize, motivate, give a little more push with the hint that there's a possible demerit or punishment if you don't.
>
> *Learn new skills.* This fresh idea is a little long-in-the-tooth, dated to another century.
>
> *Use new tech.* There is so much tech spewing forth daily that has employees gasping for air, entire enterprises have sprung up to organize all your software.
>
> *Sell through new channels.* As if that has never been thought of before.
>
> *Sell to new markets.* Really? Seriously? Haven't we heard this for decades?
>
> *Sell new products.* At the risk of diluting or downright abandoning ones that are legitimate, loved, and the bedrock of your company.

Our response? A giant yawn. Nothing new. Nothing revolutionary. Nothing connective or that could speak specifically to your organization's people as people.

We had expected to learn something new from this lightening rod of a report. How about something that we could pass along to our clients? Instead, we came away with a redirect to the age-old issue of problem-solving and hugging the Maypole of generating profits for the company.

Solving the problem in front of you doesn't get to the root cause of the less-than-stellar results you are getting. More

important, it doesn't stand as a witness to your experience—
that it is valid, has been seen, and heard.

What we've learned through decades of being in rooms
with people seeking clarity: Smart business must stop the
problem-solving. Contrary to popular business beliefs,
problem-solving has become one of the major obstacles to
business success.

STOP THE PROBLEM-SOLVING!

> My intention is to plant seeds of ideas and raise
> doubts about what we believe. Many of our beliefs
> are inherited, not opinions we have thought through.
> — Vine DeLoria, Lakota Sioux

How does **not** solving the problem work?

Consider this: A long-time client of ours, at Health and
Services (HHS),was faced with the **problem** of a significant
decrease in organ donations in the early 2000s.

After implementing the UNLearning Factor, first revealed
in the book Doug coauthored in 1994, *Enlightened Leadership:
Getting to the Heart of Change,* organ donations went from
2% to 14% in the first year.

In 2003, a major initiative was launched to increase the
number of lives saved and improved through organ and
tissue donation. It was dubbed the Donate Life Campaign,
and organ and tissue donation soared.

Of the 200 major hospitals identified by the Donate Life
Campaign in September 2003, only 26 maintained a 75%
or higher donation rate. By 2005, the number of hospitals
jumped to 185; in 2006 it increased to 371, way beyond the
200 original hospitals. By 2007, the number of hospitals in

the campaign had increased to 392 achieving 75% or higher. These phenomenal results were achieved without trying to solve the problem ... by design.

What caused the change? How did HHS guide the success?

The answer is not complicated. *The UNLearning Factor* first revealed in *Enlighted Leadership* was based on workshops Doug led prior to this book. The answer was simple: *The Process did not try to solve the problem of decreasing organ donations.*

POINT YOUR COMPASS TOWARD THE FIELD BEYOND RIGHT AND WRONG

Typically, the common approach to improving results is to start by looking for everything that is wrong with the way it is now. The next step is to find out who did it and why. Does this sound familiar?

There is already a major issue with this approach. Here's what happens. When you look for the who, what, and why of any problem, you solidify your focus to probe continually for more evidence of what has gone wrong. Who's the culprit? Why did it happen?

It is a conditioned response and a clear indication of how easily you buy into a pattern, or habit of how you get things done. Even when *all* the evidence suggests that the approach is half-assed backward.

Here's the secret equation: Your evidence is calculated in the amount of energy, plus effort, multiplied by the stress and strain divided by the anxiety required to overcome the resistance exerted by your employees so you can get to the motivation, incentives, and how-to's to fix the problems.

Are you exhausted yet? Do you see how you are in uncertain times? Here's another secret: you have always been in uncertain times. What's different today is that the uncertainty won't agree to being submerged through problem-solving. It wants a whole new ocean.

The Gartner Study we reference in this chapter includes one set of critical findings: That salespeople felt burned out; were looking for new positions; that management doesn't understand them and is disconnected from its workforce.

There was nothing new here! Basically, they are the same monumental issues that have gone unaddressed at their radical core for decades. There is a global crisis going on in corporate culture: 85% of all employees are disengaged in the workplace. How many more studies need to be published before leaders will really pay attention to the cataclysmic bottom line?

Ironically, Deloitte and Workplace Intelligence reported in 2023 that nine out of ten C-Suite leaders feel they understand their employees' well-being. On the flipside, only half agreed with them. Almost all of the leaders—2,100 in total—feel responsibility for their teams' well-being. Yet just shy of 70% reported that they did nothing to support the well-being needs of their employees.

STEP ONE Essential: Move from Problem-Solving to Solution-Finding

We say we've had all the studies we need to change the way you think about how you lead. Leaders of companies talk about their fears, about what keeps them up at night. Here's the top of that hit parade (Gartner):

Lower quota attainment
Higher burnout
Resolved or intent to leave
Shorter expected tenure

> What do you notice about this list? What is the cost to you of constantly having to motivate your sales teams?
>
> What would be the value to you and your organization if you never had to spend money to motivate your salespeople again?

From our point of view, if you were leading from an UNLearning perspective, what keeps you up at night might look more like this list:

- What do my people want beyond meeting quotas?
- What do my people need so burnout becomes a myth?
- What do my people long for in their work?
- How would making room so my people get to achieve their longings impact their decisions to build careers with my company?

What do you see as the key difference between these two lists?

WHAT'S WORKING WELL IS NOT AN ACCIDENT

Think about a recent meeting where you were the leader and you walked out feeling beat down. You rated it as the worst meeting ever because you didn't have a clear direction for the meeting. Your energy level—low. And probably more damaging, that somehow you were to blame for the confusion.

A major part of the low energy was probably caused by not much having been made clear during the meeting. Even more insidious might have been the absence of your own expertise and experience. Or maybe you convened the meeting to help generate a new direction and your expertise was falling on deaf ears.

THE TRADITIONAL APPROACH TO CHANGE

The results you are getting today are a result of doing it the way you are doing it now ... and how you did it the day before ... and the day before that and on and on.

The traditional approach used for virtually all change improvement is what causes the resistance that makes it so hard to get anything accomplished in the first place.

The traditional approach usually includes these steps:

1. Identify a problem.
2. Find an expert with a good idea.
3. Bring in an expert to tell people how to do their jobs better.
4. Overcome all the resistance caused by Steps 1, 2, and 3.

And then, the classic final step rears its head:

5. The problem remains, and possibly amplifies.

Our approach at The Institute brings common sense back to common practice.

When working with a team, it's time to ask yourself:

> From your experience, how long does it take
> for the resistance to show up when there's a
> change ordered under your leadership?

The answer we have documented from clients has always been some version of immediately!

And yet, organization after organization, boss after boss, starts with the same method that keeps proving it is going to cause resistance from the employees.

So why do most leaders repeat the same methodology when it continues to prove it isn't working? Is it a result of the need to be right rather than the desire to get it right by using the brilliance of your team?

There is another way to bring about the changes and improvements you desire with far less stress and effort. And it is easy using this premise:

Whose good ideas are people most likely to have buy-in with the least resistance?

The answer we get without fail is: their own!

In addition, what if the reason your teams aren't already doing their best work has more to do with the quality of the leadership they're provided with than a lack of expertise?

Certainly it isn't always because of poor leadership. Far too often it is a case of leaders simply doing things the way they've always been done, the traditional approach to change.

If you aren't asking your people for their input out of a desire for their ideas, you are setting up a wall of defensiveness from them.

Keep in mind, employees will become defensive and will shut down if they feel the need to defend what they are doing.

Humans are hardwired to survive. When a team's survival is in question, all the brain function training in the world won't overcome the need to protect and defend. You will see it in several ways: You'll have some fighters, some freezers, a few fleers, and many fawners. But will you have quota-raising ideas? Not one.

THE DYNAMICS OF LEADING CHANGE WITHOUT RESISTANCE

The problem-solving meeting agenda causes resistance to surface right from the start. That approach also begins with the presumption that the people just don't know how to do their work better, which in turn would obviously cause resistance. So what might be a place to start to mitigate the resistance?

Start by acknowledging team members for what they are doing right, for what they are doing that is working! Positivity.

Here are three important questions for your team members to answer.

What is working now?
Where are you already seeing the progress needed?
Where are you already getting the results wanted?

Now that you, dear leader, are acknowledging jobs well done when deserved, what are you noticing already in the level of participation in the meetings? What else are you noticing?

Congratulations. You've just addressed STEP ONE.

AMP It Up | UNLearning Lab

1. What's going to be different in a meeting that starts by acknowledging people for what they have done right and how they did it vs what they did wrong?

2. What's going to be different in the level of openness and cooperation? The sense of team and level of trust? The piece of this whole dynamic of change without resistance that seems to have been lost is this: When something is working, your teams are causing it to work.

Key UNLearnings

Leaders who believe they are responsible for motivating their people have missed the boat, literally.

✓ The results you are getting today are a result of doing it the way you are doing it now.

✓ When people are made wrong, they will shut down and become defensive. And to the degree they feel the need to defend, what else are they also doing?

✓ There are times when things are not working. And there are times when things are working. The part that seems to have slipped past our conscious awareness is that *they are both caused.*

✓ This is the message. Say it out loud: *They are both caused.*

✓ When something you're doing doesn't work, it is because the way you're doing it is causing it to not work. What seems to be missing is remembering that when it *is* working your teams are *causing* it.

6

Harvesting the Gold
from Step One

People don't resist change; they resist being changed.

What's going to be different for you and your team in a meeting that starts by acknowledging people for what they have done right vs what they did wrong?

What's going to be different in the level of openness and cooperation? Will it be the sense of team? Will it be the level of trust?

As long-time facilitators of people's transformations, we feel no need to be *right* about any of the concepts being explored here. This writing reflects the latest conclusions on our quest for getting the biggest return on investment from the energy you put into anything you do.

You still may be struggling with issues that others have figured out. Remember: Others cannot **tell** you what to do. *They don't know what to do* for anyone but themselves. They can share what worked for them, offer their experiences, but still, you will always need to experience your own wants and needs in relationship to what you are trying to accomplish.

Here's another secret hiding in plain sight: People don't resist change; they resist being changed. Noodle on that one for a few minutes and recall the number of times you've mandated any kind of change. What was your intention? What were the closed-door outcomes you were banking on?

Remember the sales organization we mentioned previously, and the sales information they affectionately referred to as the Dump Truck binders? Their year-over-year sales were abysmal. Leadership had come up with a list like the Gartner Study as to the cause of this crisis. The list was a version of the Drive and Drag model: You are either making money or you're dragging us down while you fail to make money.

Those binders were full of steps to selling, closing, and keeping their customers. They quoted sales gurus and availed themselves of the billions of dollars invested in business commandment how-to's.

Truly, it was a work of some magnitude, tabbed, with quizzes at the end of each chapter. It promised to breathe new life into the sales organization.

[*The only thing they hadn't tried was the Fellowship of the Ring®.*]

Then, they got their lowest performing teams together for a week of morning-to-night meetings as they drummed through the material.

What's your guess as to the success of the leadership's endeavor? Answer: a grueling failure for all.

The Institute got involved while Doug was flying home from D.C. Sitting next to the GM of one of the divisions, the two struck up a conversation. By the end of the trip, an invitation was issued to meet with the company's senior leadership. That meeting resulted with both of us heading to lead the national meeting the next month.

By the time they called us in, the sales teams had endearing names for us, "Gandalf and Moonbeam," because honestly, the only thing they hadn't tried was the Fellowship of The Ring. The sales teams believed it would take nothing short of magic to get them back on their feet.

They were so worn-out that they couldn't even pretend to care.

What we did:

> As soon as we arrived, we had the teams move all the schoolroom front-facing desks into a circle. Then we walked in and around between the desks and asked them to remember a time when what they were doing felt good.

Can you guess what happened? The energy in the room soared in about 10 minutes. People started sharing in noisy engagement and laughter. Guys were throwing wads of paper at each other and shouting across the room.

> Then we asked the secret sauce ... three uncomplicated questions: *What were they doing now that felt like that?* People started talking right away. They were speaking from their shared experiences—collaborating on what felt good. They were remembering really good times, times when they felt connected by a bond to do well because they liked what they did. There were nods, more laughter, and some tears.

> Then we asked: *What was leadership doing that helped them do more of what was working?* It got quiet almost instantly.

The silence propelled us to ask the big question: *What would it be worth to you to ask for what you need to make more of what's already working?* The room was so still, I wondered if anyone was breathing. Then, one by one, people started responding: "Priceless" ... "Can't quantify it!" ... "It would change our lives." They raised their hands to share until we had a room full of raised hands.

Did we need to see that amazing sight? Not nearly as much as they needed to see it. Don't get us wrong, we LOVE seeing people's geniuses come back online, but more important was the energy they felt, the motivation in each other, the energy their own answers produced. They were naming the solutions to their situation and those solutions were feeding them. With a 56% increase in sales, that quarter was the best quarter they had had in the last five quarters.

GIVE UP TRAINING IN FAVOR OF CAUSING LEARNING TO HAPPEN

We've seen this scenario multiple times in organizations. The top seller gets promoted to manager. This new manager gets thrown into the deep end of the pool, tossed a life jacket in a tome of all the selling tips and lists of what-to-do-when from Selling Gurus around the world. And now this new manager is told to produce immediately.

If they're lucky, a host of training and brilliant steps for decreasing their Drag, unlocking their inner Warrior, accessing their Vulnerability, learning to take naps, meditating under their desks, and not caving to their regret, ensue.

[*When the team resists, the manager bears down harder on the approach.*]

Training packages are big business. Most delivered online today exceed $1,200 per employee, to the tune of $87.6 billion annually per *Forbes* in its article, "How Much Are Your Disengaged Employees Costing You?" If the company is lucky, its new manager can navigate through this maze to come up with the perfect balance in the art and science of leading people.

Here is what really happens: The new manager does some pumped up version of what has always been done with a few missives from online training and sells it to the team as the reinvention of *The Way Forward*.

The manager does this because it's what he/she knows ... bringing Drive and Drag into the equation, with its hidden shame and blame mechanisms. When the team resists, the manager bears down harder on the approach. When that doesn't work, the manager starts incentivizing with whatever is on top of the Google SEO under *Increase Sellers'* **Motivation, Hunger** and **Energy** *to Close More Deals.*

If the "Expert" approach really worked, all the problems would have been solved a long time ago.

What most progressive companies do is poll salespeople for **what they want** and publish the process as the Big Fix to the problem.

What it really reenforces is that if you want to stay alive, you must Drive instead of Drag.

Study after study, similar to Glassdoor's 2023 New Hire Checklist survey, reveal one glaring and undeniable truth:

Leaders of companies are not asking their sales teams what they are engaged in that's working now, what they can do more of, better or differently to keep it working as times change. Glassdoor reports that truly thoughtful and meaningful onboarding improves retention by 82% and productivity by 70%.

Instead, they are bent on "motivating" their teams, as if the motivation must come from leaders themselves. Is any of this smacking true to you? Do you see yourself in the scenarios? What's it doing for you to admit it?

Most define "drive" and "motivation" for employees as:

> Engaged
> Persistent in the face of obstacles
> Ready to act
> Mentally alert
> Ready to take initiative

Who wouldn't want to instill that in their employees? When you see those words, doesn't it send chills all the way to your bottom line? It does ours.

When a salesperson feels the Drag, common words are:

> Procrastinate
> Feel bored
> Avoid work
> Struggle to focus
> Go through the motions

The Big Fix is clear for most employers and leaders: Reduce Drag.

[*You've got to be kidding!*]

In other words, make your team do less of avoiding, struggling, feeling bored, and procrastinating. Or, if you're the leader who likes to really take it to the extreme, tell them DON'T do those things anymore ... or else.

And, then come the four things to do instead. They are: replace your feelings that produce boredom, avoidance, struggle, and procrastination. What's missing is the critical lifeline of *How am I going to get there?*

Here's our response to the Big Fix. You've got to be kidding! This is the best being offered to people who feel burned out and on the brink? It's like offering sand to a person dying of thirst.

And here's another secret we'll share: There is NO image for not doing something. You may be asking, "What in the world does that have to do with getting rid of drag in my organization?" Here's what it has to do with: if your approach—we call it a *come-from*—is all about what your people need to stop doing, you're going to get a shock. Besides setting up the shame game, this come-from is counterintuitive because all human beings think in images. If you're telling your people to STOP doing something, or DON'T do something, the likelihood that they will be able to comply, even if they try extremely hard to accomplish the demand, is nil. They will encounter their image for DOING what you want them to stop. They will see the image for DOING what you don't want them to do.

You may say you're not visual, but you are. Your brain catalogues trillions of images throughout your life. Here's a simple example: when you tell your child, "Don't spill your juice," how long does it take before the juice is spilled? People we ask laugh and say, "... about four seconds!"

Are you getting the picture now of how dangerous focusing on problems and problem-solving is for a positive impact on your organization?

Until you get serious about alleviating the stress of burnout by caring for your employees—creating spaces for them to be seen and heard—everything you do will be a temporary fix, a band aid. And in 12 to 24 months, you'll be back here at this spot saying, "I did everything all the experts and books said would fix the problem Why isn't it working?"

Until you commit to learning how to do more of what's working well, you will be constantly fighting some kind of drag or resistance.

YOU MAY BE THE PROBLEM YOU'VE BEEN TRYING TO SOLVE

Most leaders misdiagnose the whole Drag problem as a motivation that needs to be drilled into teams. Instead, treat your salespeople holistically—as whole people—not just a means to reach your organization's goals.

In our three decades of working with organizations, there is a simple truth: Treating people as people is a paradigm-shifter. It is the gold in Emotional Intelligence and will save your company from cultural bankruptcy. This concept is the heart of our UNLearning Factor.

Don't just talk about it. Empower your people today. Release the control that you believe is yours for you alone to parlay into results.

Give people the autonomy to speak up, be heard, be seen, and to share their experience, expertise, and knowledge. The result creates explosive and exponentially positive outcomes. This is where your people begin to trust.

The sales team illustrated above came in and sat down, prepared to have the drag-to-drive points dumped on them—per usual. They were quiet, pretending to pay attention, but most were on their phones or laptops.

Our first question to them was, "What gets you out of bed every day?" Two looked up. Next, we asked, "What are the two things you'd get handled today if you were put in charge?" Silence as they looked around at each other, unsure.

Then someone said, "I'd stop these crazy unannounced store visits by our senior leadership. They feel like sneak attacks and scare the hell out of us and our stores." By the time they left the room they had changed the entire process, so it engaged all levels of store sales teams, but also took all the decisions out of the hands of headquarters. And they did it with their leadership's approval.

All we did was ask. Then we shut the hell up and listened. As we listened, a diagram was created in real time on the white board. The dots were connected live in the room so sales teams could "try on" what they were verbalizing.

Every time we do this, the effect of the process is crackling electricity. People begin to freely offer up ideas, with humor and stories and more strategic thinking, and more humor and cooperation. It never fails to bring us to our knees with gratitude. The human spirit is built to morph, and it will do so willingly to move from fear to hope.

The teams had empowered themselves to make decisions from a place of engaging their store teams, and customers out of curiosity and regard, rather than meeting a quota and memorizing the scripted decision tree. They remembered what it felt like to be motivated to find more of what's working. They were hungry to try it out together and energized to see the results.

Where do you see yourself in this scenario?

If you are saying, "I'm in the front of the room telling them how to get motivated," we're hitting the buzzer. Nice try but that's from your old playbook. It's coming from a piece of conditioning you've inherited.

[*The answer is* No.]

Most leaders are still conditioned to want to go out and tell everyone that they've found *The* Way to do it. How many times have you been in this situation? You have a problem. It doesn't matter what the problem is. You try doing it one way—no luck. Then you try another way—still not working. Then you try yet another way—still not it, and then another and another. Somewhere in all these attempts, the pieces fit, and voila! A solution emerges.

It's your solution and yours alone. You've been conditioned to believe it's your job to tell everyone else how to do your solution. Isn't that how you recognize a leader?

The answer is *No.*

If your answer was *Of course* or *Yes,* go back to the questions in STEP ONE in the previous chapter to reframe your belief system.

Part of this inherited conditioning belongs to your human need to be right, to have it figured out, to be the one with all the answers. It's a human need to make meaning of what feels like it's way out there where you can't make it matter. The discomfort can become so great you'll do just about anything to make it stop.

Sometimes it's an ego-driven approach. At The Institute, we find more often that it's a tremendous desire to connect with people. Many times, we find leaders have submerged that deep longing to connect, with the more accepted belief that the leader knows more, is smarter, has all the answers, and can make it all okay for everyone else. That they will, in essence, save their employees. Are you that savior?

AMP It Up | UNLearning Lab

1. What are you doing that's already working so well it keeps generating more excellence and innovation in your people?

2. What would be the value to you if you could stop worrying about how to motivate your people so you could get higher quotas and meet stretch goals?

3. Would you believe us if we told you if you truly cared about your people and asked them what is working well, you'd be able to focus on results?

Key UNLearnings

✓ This book reflects the latest conclusions on our quest for getting the biggest return on the investment of any energy you put into anything you do.

✓ You may be the problem you're trying to solve.

✓ Until you get serious about alleviating the stress of burnout by caring for your employees—creating spaces for them be seen and heard—everything you do will be a temporary fix, a band aid.

✓ Give people the autonomy to speak up, be heard, be seen, share their experience, expertise, and knowledge. The result creates explosive and exponentially positive outcomes. This is where your people begin to trust.

✓ It's a human need to make meaning and be right about what feels like it's way out there where you can't make it matter. The discomfort can become so great you'll do just about anything to make it stop.

✓ The human spirit is built to morph, and it will do so willingly to move from fear to hope.

7

STEP TWO: Taking the Drag Out of Your Business

There were no options. It was mandated that organizations had to be ready!

Do you want to have more things working in your life? Or do you want fewer things not working?

There's a big difference in the outcomes of these two questions.

At The Institute, we had a big awakening when we became aware of the importance of the distinctions in these two straightforward questions. It happened at the outset of a contractual engagement with a large space technology company as it faced the Y2K challenge. Because of earlier successes we'd had within the organization, it turned to us to help them find whatever solutions existed within its teams' abilities to weather both the anticipation and potential fallout from Y2K.

There were three factors to this specific issue:

1. Their organization had just contracted with an outside computer systems provider to take over ALL Information technology (IT).

2. The contract began in 1999, a short time before Y2K, the passage to the new millennium that would occur on January 1, 2000, at 12.01 a.m. as the new century began. There were no options. It was mandated that organizations had to be ready!

3. The deadline gave them only a few months to get ready to meet the 18 requirements to be Y2K compliant.

By the final week, the teams had figured out 15 of the 18 requirements necessary to be qualified by the deadline. With three more requirements to be met and running out of time, what to do? A call was made to Doug.

Doug's conclusion was that because they had been brought together only a matter of months ago to tackle a huge undertaking, the executive decision-makers of both organizations were not working well together yet. Furthermore he concluded, "You can imagine the fear, frustration, and pressure to produce fail safes while under the proverbial gun. Those factors were hampering people's abilities to access their best ideas and answers." Their creative juices were zapped, replaced by the cloud of blame that was hanging overhead.

Doug's engagement started with bringing both executive teams together. And he knew going in, that to the degree a person feels the need to protect and defend, what can you also be sure of?

The answer is embedded deep in your human psyche: when you feel a need to defend yourself, you cannot be available for anything else.

Guess what responses we get most often when we pose this scenario to any group and then ask this question: **What factors would you predict the two teams were most focused on?**

The common responses, all set up the defense and protection frame of mind and include:

- What's the problem?
- Who's to blame?
- How much did this screwup cost us?

The warrior is ready to bite back in defense if his or her position and safety is challenged.

Doug built on what had been achieved between the two teams with Step One: A look at what was working already, and what they had already achieved. And what was going well.

Through those discussions, they began to build more trust with each other and agreement and alignment with the Mission. *The old focus of what was not working was shifted to what was working.* This was the foundation for the transformation in their relationship together.

With this foundation established, the exploration now was: *What caused the successful qualification of the 15 of the 18 required areas for Y2K compliance?* Fifteen requirements had already met the desired outcomes for compliance. Now the teams were stuck on the remaining three, which were complex and layered. The language used was confusing, even for the most experienced on the team.

By applying Step Two questions to the missing three components, the teams were able to focus on what caused the first 15 to work vs focusing on what wasn't working. By applying what was working in the past, they were able to succeed with the remainder.

We tend not to be bottom-line facilitators, and in this case, here's the bottom line: As with so many of the initiatives we've been introduced to, all the essential answers were available when effective and positive questions were asked.

These were the top-line results from the teams' work together:

- Everything necessary was in place for the Y2K changeover by the deadline.

- Both executive teams were working together effectively.

- Blame and shame were replaced by collaborations and innovation.

The final three elements were completed in time to meet the Y2K deadline with both companies working together as the transition occurred.

Prior to The Institute's intervention, what factors would you predict the two teams were most focused on?

They were focused on what wasn't working ... their BIG problem ... all the problems that kept it from working ... even looking for more problems ... and how to fix those problems—real and phantom. At the same time, their eyes constantly pivoted to the ticking clock.

Before our intervention, the initial result: defensiveness and territory protection that equates to blatant resistance.

A core tenet in the way you collaborate and develop leadership in the teams you lead, no matter what industry you are in or its size, nor its prime directive, is Step Two in The UNLearning Factor. And it develops solutions quickly.

It is the shift in focus from what's wrong to what's right. The answers lead you to the next breakthrough question that is the core of Step Two: **What's causing what's working to work?**

Effective follow-up questions are now generated that include a look back at previous situations: **Where have you had issues in the past and what did you do that worked best to resolve the obstacles?**

The workplace has been conditioned to think that improvements are all about figuring out why it isn't working, whatever the "it" is. Then having to work to burnout to overcome the almost immediate resistance when a fix—usually a consultant or an expert in the perceived problem area—is imposed on the workforce.

The UNLearning Factor does a brilliant job of dissolving any resistance to change for two key reasons:

> *One, because The Institute for UNLearning does not become the experts in a client's business.* The result is that people can feel safe to lend their expertise, experience and wild and crazy ideas to the solutions process.

> *Two, The Institute does not train your people.* We cause learning to happen by allowing your people to discover their own best answers and, maybe more important—to hear them say out loud what those best answers are.

[*Outdated thinking has conditioned most people to lose conscious awareness of a very necessary and essential factor.*]

We believe your own people already have all the answers you'll ever need to build a growing and sustainable business. They need two things:

- A platform to be seen and heard.

- A platform where they can speak their truth without recrimination or punishment.

Have you provided such a platform? According to Gallup, most likely not.

Step Two is designed to mine the depths of the bench strength residing in your workforce, by giving your people permission to share their expertise, and moreover, to share what their desires are but have evaporated. Your employees know why things are working. But what often is the case, you as the leader neglect to ask them for their input.

> Outdated thinking has conditioned most leaders
> to lose conscious awareness of a very essential fact:
> There are times when things are working the way
> you want; and times when things are NOT working.
> The missing piece in your awareness is that *both*
> *are caused.*

Limiting beliefs create gaps in your conscious awareness. When it's working well, it is not an accident. It is because you are doing what causes it to work. Yet, somehow, you've been conditioned to think that it is more important to know what's causing it NOT to work, and to fix what's not working. But instead, you need to identify and focus on what is working and do more of that! Directing your attention to what isn't working does not move you forward. In fact, it diminishes your universe of possibilities.

[*All of the essential answers were already there within those who needed them.*]

Consider a situation you're facing that requires immediate progress. Instead of beginning with what's wrong, what isn't working, or what hasn't worked, begin the discussion with the questions from Step One.

The answer is always in the room. In many of the companies we've worked with, all the essential answers were already there within those who needed them.

- Where do you see focusing attention on what you don't want negatively affecting something you're working on now?

- How can you ensure that everyone is getting on board with what's going well?

- How will you connect those dots?

The answers you receive will be the foundation toward building a map of what has been done successfully to get you and your team to the current state and may already be suggesting how you have arrived at your current challenge.

Now, look at the map of everything that's working well.

STEP TWO: Taking the Drag Out of Your Business

We receive calls from leaders who are amazed at the gold they discover from asking the single question that encompasses Step Two:

What is causing what is working to work?

Can you discern the difference between this question and what we typically hear when any kind of mistake occurs?

What the hell went wrong? Who let it happen?
And how much is it costing us?

Are you thinking that these follow-up questions don't do anything to address the problem?

You're right.

The question should be designed to draw out engagement, which for you as a leader is imperative if you're going to move to the best solutions possible with everyone on board. Does that mean you're never going to ask about what went wrong and who let it happen? Of course not. But asking what went wrong at this stage will curb your team's ability to commit to forward thinking.

Questions addressing any missteps will get answered as your people are generating the-what's-next approach. By asking the Step Two questions, you are setting your team in motion to seek for the solution, which is likely to make a path to some truly innovative stuff.

This next idea is one of the very few commandments you will receive in this book:

Dear leader, do what you need to do so you avoid
getting ahead of yourself at this juncture.

The genius is arriving; just trust the process. When people feel seen and their truth is heard, they lose any fear of sharing their wildest, most fantastic, and genius-laden ideas.

Fear of recrimination, fear of demotion, of being seen forevermore as incompetent, or fringe, the silent shaming of being excluded, and that punishing interior voice that dogs you are some understandable reasons for remaining silent. Seeing a team member's idea not work straight out of the gate will very likely prevent other team members from lending their innate genius to a solution at hand.

It certainly was at the heart of what kept these combined IT teams stuck.

In the debrief with the teams after the Y2K success was acknowledged, Doug asked this question:

When you were first told about the Y2K project, was the belief that there was a way to achieve it or that there was absolutely no way to achieve it?

The entire room burst into laughter as they recalled their initial meetings. The way they explained their insight was, if you took a sheet of paper and divided it into two columns, on one side listing all the reasons you could never be successful on this task of 18 requirements in the few months to zero hour, and on the other, all the ways you could be successful, there would be an overwhelming amount of evidence that the task was completely out of reach and could never be accomplished in the allotted amount of time.

Doug's question for them at that moment was: "So, what made the difference that you are now celebrating the success?"

The answer came back: "Once you asked us what we expected of each other, we never looked at the reasons we couldn't get it done. We looked only at how to do it."

It was that simple.

It came down to the teams looking at how they would work to get the result and they kept figuring it out ... together.

Do whatever it takes for you to stay in explorer mode, asking for all the ways it's working. The difference in the answers you will receive is quantum. Because when your people are allowed to connect their own best answers, to the causes for how it's working, their whole mindset shifts to propelling forward, and outward.

Now that your team is facing the same direction, you can ask how they want to shift a misstep, that one mistake, the epic fail, so that the whole team can have more of what's working and more of what they want.

Chances are, once team members have been heard, they will willingly own where their thinking went off-track. Why? Because they want to be part of how it's going to keep working.

What's in this approach for you?

You don't have to have it all figured out before you start, or come with the solution, or stay up at night worrying if you have a team that can innovate what you need. You don't even have to figure out all the things you'll need to get the whole thing off the ground.

Just start.

Your people will carry the project forward. It's why you hired them in the first place.

Here's an example of how this works. A client we were working with was having difficulty with a number of their retail locations across the nation. Sales were slipping. They had been trying for months to turn it around.

In the first meeting with the executive team, they gushed with all the problems they had been trying to fix. They wanted us to know how hard they had been working to solve the problems. We asked if there was any place where they *were* getting the results they wanted. The instant response was, "Yes, but that's only one team! We've got all these teams where it's a mess! That's where we want you to focus."

Any chance you've lived a version of this story before?

After working for decades with teams, we noticed one similarity among them, no matter what business vertical they occupied, what generations were working together, or how they had weathered the COVID-19 Pandemic: A fascination with figuring out everything about why *things don't work.*

When we started working with the retailer, we insisted their leadership let us work *first* with the team that was succeeding. Within the first two weeks, we had another five teams looking over the fence at what we were doing, wanting to join in the shift.

There was no mandating anything. No team members were told that they had to participate.

What seems to have slipped past leaders' conscious awareness is the realization that when it is working, it is because individuals are doing what it takes to get the results they desire. At The Institute, we proceed with this basic common-sense premise: Become fascinated with understanding what will cause what is already working to work even better.

How do we do this?

It is straightforward: We assume positive intent.

What's the difference between, "How are we going to make incremental improvements?" and, "What can we do to have it work even better?"

The difference is subtle, but the power of the difference is seismic.

The difference starts with your willingness to expand your mind about what you know. It's not about changing your mind. It's about being willing to stretch your understanding.

When you live in a world of incremental improvements, what are you sure to be surrounded by?

Problems. Problems that need fixing with more incremental improvements.

We see it often. People tightly focused on making another improvement along an already deeply grooved track, typically ignoring the juggernaut of innovation that is off the beaten track.

[*That's the power of having the creator-leader mindset.*]

What you gain is pure potential when you move your questions to a world of, "What's causing it to work, and what can we do to have it keep working seamlessly ... to exceed the task at hand?" You become surrounded by employees who already know what will work.

Because while you're up in the middle of the night worrying about what might break next, your teams are dreaming up solutions from that oh so radical space—the one where they are creating systems that make what you're worried about obsolete.

You can feel it in their energy, their desire to collaborate and their hunger to see what will work this time.

You notice that it's not the hunger to get more sales, beat the other guy, or put your competition out of business. Rather, it's the hunger to innovate, to create, to build something that no one has thought of before and to feel the quantum energy that comes from doing it together.

That's the power of having the creator-leader mindset. You hold the space open for your teams to flourish. You get up every day and let your focus be to remove all obstacles keeping your people from putting their wildest ideas to work.

Try being the servant to an innovative environment for a minute. Let them figure out where the cogs go. Next month you won't need cogs anymore. They will have figured out something you haven't dreamed of yet.

You are now in what we like to refer to as "the wild blue yonder" of possibilities.

And here's the best news for you. You don't have to spend loads of money to train and retrain and coax and incentivize your best talent to stay. Because when you ask them the questions in Step One and Step Two, you make the first in a series of human experiences: You open the field of trust.

Imagine running a company that no longer uses the dirty dozen of terms: retention, termination, stress management, disengagement, probation, compliance, right, wrong, good, bad, human capital, and the new darlings around the water cooler—quiet quitting and the ascension of AI.

And we're only getting started. Other commonplace phrases define how we think of people and their relationship to work: *our policy, unlimited earning potential, competitive pay, pay parity, in the trenches, many hats, savvy powerhouse, rock star, works well under pressure,* and the latest ... *quiet firing.*

Building trust by using Step Two begins to dissolve the resistances that put words like compliance and terminate in the corporate lexicon in the first place.

If you don't believe us, what's keeping you from believing the majority of today's workforce is actively practicing disengagement?

This single statistic is telling us we have passed the time when all we had to do was to keep getting better at the way we've always done it. Because that outdated thinking will not produce what you truly want and need now.

Nowhere may this evolving awareness be more important to understand than its impact on what it now means for you to be an effective leader.

AMP It Up | UNLearning Lab

1. What's keeping you from building a robust engagement strategy for your teams?

2. Do you believe there can be change without resistance?

3. Do you believe that incremental improvement is the key to increasing profitability?

4. Choose a time you mandated a system-wide change. How much resistance surfaced when it was introduced? What did you do to overcome the resistance? What worked and what did not?

Key UNLearnings

✓ Any and all the essential answers will be available when effective and positive questions are asked.

✓ Limiting beliefs create gaps in your conscious awareness.

✓ Do whatever it takes for you to stay in explorer mode by asking for all the ways it's working.

✓ You don't have to have it all figured out before you start, or come with the solution, or stay up at night worrying if you have a team that can innovate what you need.

✓ Once team members have been heard, they will willingly own where their thinking went off-track because they want to be part of how it's going to keep working.

✓ Get up every day and let your focus be to remove all obstacles keeping your people from putting their wildest ideas to work.

✓ Building trust by using Step Two begins to dissolve the resistances that put words like *compliance* and *terminate* in the corporate lexicon in the first place.

8

Harvesting the Gold from Step Two

*If you're faking stewardship with your employees,
trust us, they know. And, what's more, you know.
It's what really keeps you up at night.*

The place you live from will be your most powerful tool
in the future of your business, and in the future of doing
business.

At The Institute, we refer to it as your *come-from*.

Your come-from is your most treasured and influential
tool. It's a little like Honor. It can't be taught, but you know
when you don't have it. When you do have it, it becomes the
gold standard for how you do everything.

When we show up in a room full of your teams, we ask
questions. We avoid telling, but rather pose possibilities and
concepts that follow our questions. We view our approach as
being constantly curious, without forming any opinions or
judgments beforehand. In fact, one of the things we ask your
teams right away: Start noticing how often you frame your
interactions using descriptors such as good or bad, better or
worse, right or wrong.

They are costly words because of the power of their
impact depending on a person's history with them: A parent

whose praise or disapproval was wrapped around "good" or "bad."

"Why can't you be more like your sister? She's so good?"

We come with all compassion for the pain you and your employees feel. We listen to what is being expressed, and maybe more important—what's not being expressed. We witness the truth coming to light in the room. Your employees' answers are heard because we never assume the role of the expert. They are the experts. When they get to be seen and heard, they feel cared for and that's when the truth starts to influence all the decisions that get made. It's when trust begins to drive the process.

ENGAGEMENT AND YOUR BOTTOM LINE

Does engagement matter? Is it a fad word or a true trend? Here are the statistics we've provided throughout the book, and they illustrate a staggering picture. According to Gallup, your employee engagement is a factor and one that you as a leader ignore at your company's peril and your own.

> Employees who find a passion and purpose at work are more than three times more likely to stay with their organizations than those who don't.

> Engaged employees reduce absenteeism by 41%.

> Highly engaged businesses achieve 59% less turnover.

> Highly engaged employees result in a 23% increase in profitability.

> 85% of employees are most motivated when internal communications are effective.

90% of leaders believe if they fully engaged their employees, they would increase profitability.

25% of businesses succeed in designing an engagement program.

With the majority of today's employees practicing the art of disengagement, what does that mean for you, your employees, and your business?

According to Gallop, employees saying the chief de-incentivizers in their work environments are (drags on performance) are:

1. Lack of development opportunities in the organization (51%)

2. Feeling like a cog in a big machine (44%)

3. Vague, unactionable manager feedback (33%)

4. Administrative burden (27%)

What's one thing you notice as you read the list? What are they telling you in very clear terms? Here's a clue: Every single one of those indicators refers to a *feeling*.

Your employees feel unseen and unheard.

Let's pause for a moment here. Ask yourself, how have you felt when you weren't valued?

If you are ready to lead without resistance, and are less focused on keeping your teams motivated and hungry, and more focused on galvanizing your teams' time and energy, what will happen to how your employees feel?

What would be the value to you as a leader if you didn't have your teams handling administrative paperwork 50% of the time? Would it be like keeping a racehorse in the barn half its life?

Well ... no, yet it does create a powerful mental picture as an illustration of performance drag.

Now reread the list of four drags on performance above.

What do they have in common?

All of them are guided by and impacted by a leader. If you're faking stewardship with your employees, trust us, they know. And, what's more, you know. It's what really keeps you up at night.

So, the first deduction we made is that there's a heavy shadow being cast over the role of a leader.

Here's an eye-opening statistic to chew on: 82% of *Workers Would Consider Quitting Their Jobs Because of a Bad Manager*. In November 2021, a record **4.5 million** U.S. workers quit their jobs.

In its "State of the Global Workplace" report, Gallup concludes that "85% of employees are not actively engaged or (are) actively disengaged at work." As a leader, how effective would your company be if only 15% of employees are actively engaged?

The collective toll on your bottom line for that little statistic is a cool $450—$550 billion annually.

Data show that a disengaged employee costs an organization approximately **$3,400 for every $10,000 in annual salary.**

CRACKING THE NUT ON INCREMENTAL IMPROVEMENTS

Let's take a break from the staggering reality of these statistics to deliver some good news.

All this is infinitely resolvable.

What's required, dear leader, is your willingness to look at what you've been doing. If you're pretty happy with the incremental improvements you and your senior team have instituted, you really need to read this section carefully.

Are you experiencing any fallout from a disengaged workforce? If yes, what can help you crack this nut is understanding that **incremental improvements** is another term for "Box checked. I don't have to pay attention to this."

Essentially what you're doing in this scenario is running on automatic, coasting, and letting the belief systems you've held for years continue to guide your decisions and actions.

What we recommend: Take a break from having to know it all and control it all. If you report to a Board, consider what works best in that relationship for your employees, and be brave about asking your Board for that.

Allow your present moment awareness to surface as revealed in Chapter One, *Awareness.* What's actually happening to your employees? It is time to stop talking, driving, and deciding, long enough to let your people be seen and heard. Furthermore, they need to be seen and heard in such a way that there won't be any retribution for their having opposed the current popular trend, often promoted by you ... their leader.

Here's another precept of our work that we covered in Chapter One, *Step One* and believe it's worth repeating: Whose ideas are people most like to buy into first? The undisputed answer: Their own!

The discussion usually brings nervous laughter in the room as the realization begins to sink in: How easily most have become conditioned to follow an automatic set of behaviors, tow the party line and put the company sacred cows on a pedestal that should have been wrapped in fishmonger paper and discarded long ago. Normalized acceptance of inappropriate behaviors, policies, and corporate politics guarantee employee disengagement as they struggle to maintain them.

Recently, we were approached by a large organization with a global presence. They needed our help because they were experiencing mounting attrition.

We were clear with them: Stop the problem-solving and start showing up. Live in real-time with your employees. If you do that, and really mean it, you won't have to figure out how to turn every single cog in your vast machine.

Their answer: "We know you're right and we believe you. We just don't have the time." "Not enough time" is one of the costliest sacred cows used to maintain the status quo in companies today.

In the next few pages, we're going to give you the most important information in our UNLearning Factor to galvanize a team of two or two thousand.

HUMAN POTENTIAL

The inside scoop on how to make your energy work for quantum results.

Think for a moment about this question: Are you at your best when your energy level is high? Or is your energy level high when you're at your best?

[*The good energy is going to run out. It always does.*]

The executive teams we work with often come to pretty much the same conclusion in answering that question. The two are so interwoven that it's a lot like *which came first, the chicken or the egg*. At The Institute, it doesn't matter which came first. The key to energy is first noticing it and then doing more of what "it" is to generate more of what's working. We often ask, "How do you know when the energy drains?" The resounding answer comes back from the room, "When it starts to suck!"

One thing for sure is when you're living and operating in a high-energy state, you are better at what you do. And you tend to get more done with less stress and effort. You feel as if you are in the zone and everything is flowing. It's as if you can't make a false move or misstep.

When we were working with one of the U.S. Armed Forces, we heard this from a team leader,

> I love it when my team is in the groove. Everything just flows. But I'm constantly afraid of ways the other shoe is going to drop, and it'll start sucking again. In fact, I start looking for all the ways it's going to fail.

What belief system is alive in this leader's thinking? We've seen it countless times and most likely so have you: The good energy is going to run out. It always does.

What if part of being a great leader is looking for all the ways to keep the energy flowing in your people? The answer is again simple: Let them decide the degree they need. Make it your job to ensure they have as many access points as possible for energy to flow, both individually and collectively.

If the above is not ringing true for you, this may be a place to stop and review.

Where is your own leadership style conflicting with what is being suggested in these pages?

What do you feel is unimportant or negligible?

On what points are you saying to yourself something like: "Yeah, may work for your teams, but not mine!"

What lie are you telling yourself to keep the status quo?

The straightest path to empowering and directing this energy is exactly the opposite of what you have learned to do to gain success and improvement. In fact, the ways you've been conditioned to implement improvement and change are a major cause of misguided effort and stress.

UNLearning: Leading Change without Resistance is being written as much for us as it is for you. At The Institute, we learn by reflecting on our experiences and interactions with teams. Each one is unforgettable. We come out of every engagement altered in ways we could never have imagined going into them. For us, we're never moving toward a destination, but rather a deeper insight, fresh eyes on a well-worn subject. We're continually thrilled and enlightened by the brilliance of the unexpected that so many individuals bring.

The source of that transformative energy is not complex. We go in to make a safe container, and then we just pay attention, really deep attention. Questions are asked that come out of a curiosity about the people we're engaging. We ask about what hasn't been said in the room before.

We impart our UNLearning Factor to every organization we work with. And they experience their own personal and cultural transformations within their teams while we are there and after we leave. It's nothing we can foresee. It's never the same way twice. It takes an incredible amount of awareness and courage because we stand in the I-don't-know space almost all the time. What makes it courageous is that we live and work in a corporate cultural environment that still prizes the one-who-knows-it-all: the smooth talker, the one who has snappy soundbite answers for every question asked.

DIAGNOSE, DESIGN, DEVELOP

Consultants and the media embrace the fix-it mentality with advice bites so succinct and box checkable. But it's time to dump the posturing.

Instead, let the people on the front lines drive the learning. Let them diagnose, design and develop based on what's already working; what they are doing to cause it to work; what they want more of; and what they need to have to get it done.

After thirty years of being in rooms with people, the number one factor that's gone to hell most often in the organization is communication: the lack of it; the miscommunication of it; even the nil of it. There are now as many as five generations sharing workplaces and people are failing miserably at communication: They don't do enough of it; they misread one another; they form cliques; they make assumptions. And then, they get resentful and tight-lipped, start taking things personally, stop doing their best, and stop keeping their word.

Does this sound like your company?

When your people come to you with their list of what they need to keep doing more of what's working, make it your mission to make sure they have what's on their lists. Then make some agreements about how they will get back to you with results. Do not revert back to telling them all the reasons they can't have something or how they need to comply.

Can you commit to doing that?

Communicating has two sides: the speaker and the listener. Can you hear what is being said? Do you understand what is being said? Listen closely. Come a little closer. Just a little more ... now can you hear that loud and clear?

It's the sound of no one complaining, resisting, bad-mouthing, or quitting.

It's the sound of alignment, agreement, cooperation, and no drag.

It's the process your people went through to get to their own answers, not the answers the expert came up with.

This logic is all based on a couple of simple premises. The first is the answer to the question: "Whose ideas are people likely to buy into first?" In asking this of thousands of people over thirty years, there still has been only one answer: "Their own."

The second is the answer to the question: "How many of your own great ideas have you ever resisted?" Only one answer in over thirty years has been volleyed back: "NONE."

The more often you notice when you make conscious choices instead of automatically doing what you've always done, possibilities and options open up and expand.

It's like a great flowering of connectivity.

Our intent is not to teach anything. Our intent is to create a shared remembering. It is to lead you to deeper levels of clarity on the only answers that count—your own. If we do anything at The Institute, we cause learning to happen.

You can think of it as a reconnection with some common-sense beliefs that have fallen by your wayside but could serve you now if you are willing to unlearn what's no longer working. Separate those outmoded ways of operating from what you truly desire. Only then can you make clear choices about what you want to do—manifesting your deep desires.

Sometimes it seems we get away from what we do know. At The Institute we like to refer to the term "to educate," which comes from the Latin word *educare*—to draw forth from.

Have you been conditioned to translate education to mean, "The instructor is at the front of the room, has all the answers for you, and will drill them into you."?

- What are you ready to let go of?
- Are you ready to make room for what's next?
- Step Three is next: What you think you know.

AMP It Up | UNLearning Lab

1. If your desire is to have more things working more often, what might you want to know more about?

2. What are the biggest insights for you from the answers from your people, and how do you intend to reflect their solutions back so they know you are with them?

3. What is showing up for you that there can be change without resistance?

4. How does this demonstrate that there can be change without resistance?

5. When posed with a challenge, what do you notice as your first reaction?

6. How important is it that your people get acknowledged when doing well?

Key UNLearnings

✓ If you're faking stewardship with your employees, trust us, they know. And, what's more, you know. It's what really keeps you up at night.

✓ The place you live from, your come-from, will be your most powerful tool in the future of your business, and in the future of doing business.

✓ Avoid telling, but rather pose possibilities and concepts that follow your questions. It's a form of

being constantly curious, without forming any
opinions or judgments beforehand about what and
who is good, or bad, better or worse, right or wrong.

✓ The more often you notice when you make conscious
choices instead of automatically doing what you've
always done, possibilities and options open up and
expand.

✓ Reconnect with some common-sense beliefs that
have fallen by your wayside but could serve you
now if you are willing to unlearn what's no longer
working.

✓ Separate those outmoded ways of operating from
what you truly desire. Only then can you make clear
choices about what you want to do—manifesting
your deep desires.

9

STEP THREE: The Answer Is Always in the Room

Step Three questions are likely to cause a crash of mythic proportions.

You're always moving toward getting more of something. Our question is: How do you know when it is what you truly want?

Step Three is about asking questions that move the conversation to pressure testing: a strategy of identifying what you think you know.

All the questions at this stage need to be focused on and directed to clarifying your goals, the outcomes and accomplishments, and any results you want to produce.

This is where it gets tricky for you, the leader. If you have been operating from a double agenda, your own, and the one you prop up for the team and organization, Step Three questions are likely to cause a crash of mythic proportions. In other words, the truth will come out. It's a good thing.

You will not be able to maintain a secret purpose while investing in the success of your teams. If you believe you've been able to manage it successfully up until now, we'll bet you also are witnessing:

- diminished engagement in your workforce

- very little, if any innovation

- flagging commitment

- increased sick days

- excessive mid and senior level departures

- a bottom-line graph that looks like a mighty roller coaster

This checklist of issues is not a pretty thing to observe or be a participant in.

[*What secret agenda are we talking about?*]

Is the checklist above eerily similar to your situation? We promise that we're not gazing into a crystal ball with your company's name on it. We're coming from decades of witnessing the outcomes of misaligned missions and agendas from leaders who claim they want what's best for their workforce, yet do absolutely nothing to uphold, support, or enhance their teams' abilities to be successful.

Time's up.

It's time to pay the piper and either get your agenda aligned unequivocally with the stated goals and outcomes of your company's Mission or do what so many leaders do: Ride the wave until it wipes you out.

And it will wipe you out.

If you're holding on for dear life right now, chances are good that your secret agenda is apparent to everyone around you. You're the only one who believes it's a secret.

What secret agenda are we talking about? It's the one that is driving all of your most important leadership decisions. So, instead of being kept up at night by how well your employees are engaged and collaborating, this one has you panicked.

Some secret agenda items could include:

- The one that's tied to your bonus.
- The one that dumps a boatload of stock at a deep discount price into your portfolio.
- The one where your Board's rock-solid belief in your abilities is untouchable.
- The massive golden parachute hanging over your head.
- The golden handcuffs that you're not sure you want the keys to.
- The bevy of perks you consider priceless that you don't want to let go of.
- The hefty raise tied to performance that has you in nightly sweats at 2:30 a.m. asking yourself how you're going to whip your teams into shape so they deliver the numbers you need.
- The personal financial obligations you incurred with the promise of the wave.
- The internal quota that you have set for yourself.

[*It's the pay-now or pay-later plan.*]

If you're ready to unlearn that death grip you have on what your life is supposed to look like, and really get on the side with your employees, read on. It will be your lifeline when the wave crashes.

THE ANSWER IS ALWAYS IN THE ROOM

There are two key factors that influence the impact of this important step in your exploration.

> **One**—before focusing on clarifying the desired objective, what is your sense of the benefits gained from the questions in Step One and Step Two?

Rather than lead with what isn't working and who is to blame, it's much easier to accomplish any objective built on a foundation of agreeing on what works and what causes it to work.

> **Two**—is the freedom from the all-too familiar practice of you, the leader, stating the goal, then conclude by asking something like, "everybody clear on what we're doing?"

With your willingness to take the time to hear each team member, what do you see as the most important benefits of using this approach?

[*Fixing all the problems from the past will have you in retro-motion.*]

It's the pay-now or pay-later plan.

Think of what a few moments of clarity at the beginning of a project can save in frustration later. Step Three has nothing to do with good people vs bad people or more capable people vs less capable people. Step Three has everything to do with allowing your team to be seen and heard.

Using the combined power of answers from the first three steps, you are continuously clarifying *your intentions,* and where team members need to put *their attention.* Getting from where you are to where you want to be is the continuous goal. At this stage, focusing attention on fixing all the problems from the past will have you in retro-motion where you will lose momentum and the attention and energy of your team.

Ask the question:

**What do we need to know about what didn't work
to help us get to our goal?**

It is far more strategic and is going to get your team much more engaged than asking the common five questions that lead to tanking a team and everyone thinking that they must have answers to them.

AVOID asking these five common questions that lead to tanking a team!

1. What didn't work?
2. Who failed?
3. Why didn't it work?
4. How much did this screw-up cost us?
5. And our all-time favorite: Whose fault is it?

Our truth ... these questions are worthless at best and damaging in the creation of true engagement. At this point in the process, the only question worth asking will evoke collaboration and engagement ....

What do we need to know about what didn't work to help us get to our goal?

A common tendency is to want to get right to the action that will alleviate the pain and suffering caused by the way you asked the questions. When humans are shamed, blamed, and put on the defensive, what else can they be doing at the same time?

The answer is clinically based: Nothing ... absolutely nothing.

To the degree your people feel they need to defend and protect, they will be unable to move into any kind of solutions-based thinking where they are able to collaborate progressively and creatively.

There is a vital step in between, another key of the "pay-now or pay-later plan" that is generated right here.

The all-important and essential in-between question raises its head. Our work has shown that the opportunity surfaces for prework: asking team members what they want or desire. When asked with a come-from of curiosity, it's one of those scenarios that always works when approached with fully engaged deep listening.

A great example was when The Institute worked with a gentleman who headed up a federal agency. When he was promoted to district director, he called a meeting with his new staff. All he knew coming in was this: As one of ten district commanders across the country, each was responsible for enforcement of all U.S. regulations for that agency in his/her designated district. He wanted to create the space for his team to work together collectively in order to achieve its Mission.

They came to the meeting prepared to defend themselves, with files, charts, and reasons why things were the way they were, and the excuses they needed to absolve themselves from the aspects of their work over which they had little or no control. Everyone figured the new district director was going to do the typical new leader speech, "I'm the new boss. Here are all the things I see that are wrong, and here's how we (you) are going to start doing things to fix them."

It's every mid and senior manager's nightmare: New initiatives that bump into old ones, ill-conceived and quickly executed processes that lead to confusion, dissatisfaction, and resistance. But because he had had such positive past results using The UNLearning Factor, he started the meeting differently. He asked for participation before the meeting ever got started.

In advance of the meeting, he asked each of his direct reports to come prepared to share two or three things that were working the best in his or her respective department. In addition, they were asked to report on what they would like to do differently to further their leadership capabilities, and how they would like to improve their department. He asked them to include how each change would create the results they desired most.

The direct reports were incredibly energized by this approach. Because they were able to share their goals and objectives, where and how they would focus their attention, results were immediate. And an added bonus to this approach: Because they were sharing their objectives with one another, they were collaborating. In doing so, they enhanced results and their sustainability.

As they shared their learnings with one another—what they were doing to cause it to work—they were able to reach their desired results. Along with continued discoveries of what they were doing that was working best, they shared how their teams had no resistance to any of the changes that they were implementing.

Here's the secret that bears repeating in every chapter of *UNLearning*:

People don't resist change; they resist being changed.

Involve them in discovering which changes they believe are important and how to effectively implement them. When you let your people drive the learning, you'll have a workforce that is building a healthy culture and a healthy business.

The success story we've relayed here would not have been possible without his initial clarity. This leader wanted his new team to be fully engaged in any shifts they would make. He made himself clear at the start. He was not the typical boss coming in with all the answers, all the judgments about what had been going on, and how he was going to save them with his great ideas and strategies.

An essential shift-in-thinking is possible once you establish clarity among your team(s). And, once there is agreement and alignment about where you are headed, your job becomes simple: Get all the barriers out of your team's way ... *including you.*

If you were to ask your team members today what their understanding is of one of your goals or objectives, how close do you think they would be in their agreement?

- Are they in alignment?
- How close to your specific goal are they?

[*They didn't work then ... and they won't work now.*]

There is, perhaps, no more costly belief today than the belief that there is only one best way to achieve a goal.

If you're a leader who believes that every one of your people hears what you say in the same way just because you are the one saying it, take this opportunity right now and unlearn this conditioned thinking. It's the conditioning that has you believing that the one at the head of the table, with the biggest office, is the one who has to have all the answers and is the smartest person in that room.

So wrong.

The generation of agreement and alignment is accomplished by simply asking each member to share his/her understanding of what is being asked.

Give it a shot. See what happens. If nothing changes, do it again. Your dumbed down team didn't happen overnight. Give the team a few go arounds. Do not regress and embrace your old ways! They didn't work then ... and they won't work now.

Here's a clue: Engage each person early and often. We're stunned again and again when we see leaders say something to this effect: They've been waxing on about the greatness of their latest brain-child plan, and then once all the air has been sucked out of the room, they look up and say, "Everyone understand where we're headed?" or "Make sense?"

Do you recognize yourself in this scenario? If you do, what's one thing you could do differently to make sure everyone is in agreement?

Fixing Doesn't Work.

When we say, *fixing doesn't work,* do we mean don't bother with attending to issues and challenges that need to be adjusted, recalibrated, or discarded? Absolutely not. Any implementation is going to need constant adjustments, with the key word being "constant." Processes, like people, evolve. Your team members' understanding of *what* and *how* is going to evolve as they collaborate to implement their design. What they intend to do is going to be where they focus their attention.

So, getting crystal clear on what the desired outcome needs to be at the outset, so that everyone involved has a stake, is ground-zero critical. If you don't have complete buy-in, you're going to be going back to do a lot of what you've always done: fixing problems.

And fixing problems, while it looks good on a quarterly balance sheet and your Board of Directors meetings, does nothing to enhance culture, deepen employee commitment, or uplevel collaboration. In fact, it does the opposite. It dehumanizes connection, burns your team out, and gets the blame and shame game going at full tilt.

AMP It Up ⚡ | UNLearning Lab

1. What's one indication you have right now that your leadership style isn't working?

2. Again, it's putting common sense into common practice. How will you know when it's the best time to determine if all agree on what is desired?

3. What are you ready to release in your own leadership style to make room for a culture that has your employees thriving?

Key UNLearnings

✓ You're always moving toward getting more of something. Our question is: How do you know when it is what you truly want?

✓ You will not be able to maintain a secret purpose while investing in the success of your teams.

✓ Time's up ... you can't ride the wave forever. And a wise leader knows that wave-riding should not be done as a solo venture.

✓ To the degree your people feel they need to defend and protect, they will be unable to move into any kind of solutions-based thinking where they are able to collaborate progressively and creatively.

✓ Getting crystal clear on what the desired outcome needs to be at the outset, so that everyone involved has a stake, is ground-zero critical.

✓ Fixing problems does nothing to enhance culture, deepen employee commitment or uplevel collaboration. It dehumanizes connection, burns your team out, and gets the blame and shame game going at full tilt.

10

Harvesting the Gold from Step Three

A good leader understands it's his/her employees' engagement that creates wild success. A good leader is interested in how each employee is contributing. And a good leader envisions how each employee will contribute in the future.

How Change Really Happens

Any real change implies the breakup of the world as one has always known it, the loss of all that gave one an identity, the end of safety. And at such a moment, unable to see and not daring to imagine what the future will now bring forth, one clings to what one knew, or dreamed that one possessed. Yet, it is only when a man is able, without bitterness or self-pity, to surrender a dream he has long possessed that he is set free, he has set himself free for higher dreams, for greater privileges.

— James Baldwin, *Nobody Knows My Name*

The belief that your leader-built, all-by-yourself plan brings something new just by your having brought it into existence as the leader is a belief we hope to help move toward its final death spiral.

The second part of the all-by-yourself plan involves you getting your teams trying harder to make work what's proving it isn't working even after fixing a myriad problems. It is a model that has seen its day, and frankly, in our estimation is largely responsible for a two-decade low in employee engagement.

The misguided belief that a good leader will make his/her plan successful by fixing problems and putting out fires is ridiculous. And turning a plan that doesn't have full buy-in into a sacred cow to save your Leader Legacy is pure folly. Just ask the 85% of globally disengaged workers. We keep harping on it, but the number hasn't budged in decades. That's a sad indictment on the state of leadership today.

Perhaps the truest role a great leader plays is in modeling *being*. For it is from the place of being that true collaboration and best heart-led practices can be cocreated.

Heaven forbid we mention the words "being" and "heart-led" in a book made for business. But we're doing it. And we're doing it because it's high time we put heart-led leadership front and center.

What do you think we mean when we say heart-led?

> *Be in the service of your people's success. If anything keeps you up at night, make it that you are seeking more ways to remove barriers standing in the way of your people's collaborative energy.*

Do that and you'll never have to motivate, incentivize, or coax innovation again.

You cannot be aligned with your purpose and the well-being of your employees if you are not 100% engaged in being in service to their success. And to be of service to another human being, you must lead with your competence, skill, knowledge, experience, and expertise. But if all that acumen doesn't pass through the heart, it will never, not ever become wisdom.

That's really your only job ... ever.

[*You know it's coming.*]

Make sure your people have what they need by asking them what it will take to make it work, whatever that "it" is. You'll be amazed at how occupied you'll become re-envisioning with your teams, all the processes and systems so that you're focused on doing more of what's working. You'll be even more amazed at the high level of engagement when everyone is fully in on the outcome and knows what s/he is doing to contribute.

A heart-led leader is interested in how each employee is contributing to the bottom line, of course, but first, to each one's sense of worth and well-being. As a leader if you do that, you'll have a workforce that is indefatigable.

What world would we be living in where leading with heart was worth millions? Would you like to hazard a guess at what you'd be worth as a leader by making sure, before anything else, that your teams are well-cared for? Here's a guess from us: rich beyond measure.

The day of the haves vs the have-nots is experiencing a tremendous swell. Whether it comes to a tumultuous end, we don't know. The day of the awares vs the aware-nots is on the rise. It's a wave you can either get on board to ride or let it pass you by as you get tossed in the churn.

You know it's coming. It's why you are up night after night. Something is bothering you and you cannot put your finger on it. And worse, nothing you've ever used successfully is quite working anymore. Trust it. It's trying to lead you to your own best answers, ones you've never voiced before.

AMP It Up | UNLearning Lab

1. What would it take to generate wealth based on how much you care about who is doing the doing that makes the widgets you produce?

2. What world would you be living in where leading with heart was worth millions?

3. Would you like to hazard a guess at what you'd be worth as a leader by making sure, before anything else, that your teams are well-cared for?

4. If you like this question, you'll enjoy the questions in Step Four and Step Five coming up.

Key UNLearnings

✓ A good leader understands it's his/her employees' engagement that creates wild success. A good leader is interested in how each employee is contributing. And a good leader envisions how each employee will contribute in the future.

✓ Perhaps the truest role a great leader plays is in modeling *being*. For it is from the place of *being* that true collaboration and best heart-held practice can be cocreated.

✓ The day of the awares vs the aware-nots is on the rise. It's a wave you can either get on board to ride or let it pass you by as you get tossed in the churn.

11

STEP FOUR:
It's Always in the ASK

The difference in how your people engage is seismic.

At this point in the process, what's your sense of the importance and need to invest time exploring Step Four?

Whether consciously aware of it or not, there is a "why" behind everything we do, every decision we make. Your "why" is your intention. Clarity on the *why* impacts how much or how little you invest, apply yourself to achieving your desired outcome. This is true for you individually, and for you and your team collectively.

Our experience continues to reveal a far-too-frequent pattern among those responsible for producing desired results. The pattern we recognize is outdated and well past time to *unlearn*. It is the belief that you, the leader, assumes everyone on the team is clear about the importance of doing what you're setting out to do.

No wonder only 15% of employees worldwide are engaged at work.

Based on this erroneous assumption, leaders bypass this essential factor. Does this include you? Are you taking the time required to make sure everyone has the same map for moving forward?

One of the primary contributing factors to your team's disengagement and resistance comes from how much you believe that because you came up with the idea, everyone should arrive at the same conclusion. This belief is a costly one. You are missing most of the big picture because you've just disengaged 85% of your team.

What impact does understanding why you're doing something have in the way you apply yourself to getting it done? Think about it. If you believe you don't have time to get clear with your team by asking the Step Four question, what makes you think you'll make the time to go back and redo it when it gets screwed up?

To say nothing of ...

- the cost
- the time wasted
- the demoralization of your team
- the need to motivate and redouble efforts, and
- the requirement to overcome the resentment caused when you didn't ask the questions the first time around.

The cost is devastating.

Your job becomes making sure you have created time and space for the questions that follow here. They need to be asked, and more important, to be answered. It's not nearly as important for you to hear the answers as it is for your team to hear their own answers.

When your team members hear themselves out loud, this process increases their capacity for collaboration and cocreation. You just might bust the silo effect with it.

You become a better leader not by having the best answers but by getting the best answers from your people. Your big shift will be in your willingness to manage your listening skills.

It's time to pull up a chair and take some notes after you ask this question:

What will be the benefit when you achieve your goal?

[*Clueless, bobbling heads disappear.*]

Again, this is not the place for you, the leader, to tell your people what the benefit will be. This is the place to ask them! Asking them could include these follow-up questions:

Who will benefit most?
What will be the benefit to customers?

At this stage in the process, it may also be prudent for you to ask:

What will be the cost if we don't achieve our goal?

Asking follow-up questions becomes especially important when there is significant impact to your people if they don't reach the objective. When you ask your team, "Is everybody clear about what I want?" the deer in the headlight reaction can be what you receive, or a bunch of bobbling heads who are clueless but are attempting to appease you.

Either way, how your people apply themselves to what they are doing is a direct result of their understanding of *why* they're doing it. It's the classic WII-FM – "what's in it for me?" approach that is usually waffling through their

minds every time you come up with something new.
Its impact on your people is directly related to their level
of engagement ... always.

Where you pay attention matters so you can then create
an intention that is inclusive. With clear intentions, people
can focus their attention with great clarity. Clueless, bobbling
heads disappear.

[*We are all moving toward something all the time.*]

There is nothing more important than being clear from
the outset about what you want—your desired outcome.
By asking the questions, your team drives their collective
understanding of what is *being* accomplished. The answers
they produce lead them to a deeper knowing of what it will
take to get it done. Through the process, they understand
what their individual contributions will be, and how they
connect to each other.

Guess what? You've just achieved 80% of how to lead
change without resistance. It's not complicated.

We are all moving toward something all the time.
We have no choice ... nor do you. The distinction you can
make as a leader is in your ability to consciously choose
what you want to keep moving toward, which means you
better know what you want! And even more important,
you have got to know what your team needs and wants to
be successful.

If you're not clear, you'll default to what you've always
done to get what you've always had. How has that worked
for you? What you are focused on determines what you

will keep getting more of as you move toward it ... over ... and over ... and over.

Are you recognizing yourself in this scenario?

So much of the conditioning you have inherited is focused on what you don't want and will do almost anything to avoid. Then, you focus on what to worry about so you can continue to keep avoiding what you don't want.

But continually focusing on what you don't want keeps you from the real gold.

In our facilitating sessions, we observe how leaders want to move very quickly from a problem to an action—a fix—without taking the time to ask employees what they are clear about, and what their options are.

[*As a leader, it becomes your sworn duty to pause.*]

Typically, once you've laid out the problem, and its fix, we hear a leader ask some version of this question, "Is everyone clear?" or, "Does this make sense?" Questions asked ... are you ready to get responses ... or questions fired back at you? How many times have you seen a room explode with raised hands clamoring to voice their questions?

If your answer is not often, or never, you'd be in the majority.

THE POWER OF THE PAUSE

Your power as a leader is to pause long enough to ask, "*What* is clear here?" or "*How* is this making sense?" To make a practice of this approach, you must be able to slow down, and pause. People need time to catch up in their minds.

As a leader, it becomes your sworn duty to pause. Your UNLearning is in your capacity to ask "what" and "how."

As facilitators, one of our signatures is in our willingness to *pause* ... often. We will be facilitating a conversation, while also tracking on multiple levels, from the energy in the room, to the dilation of team members' pupils. We are constantly listening and watching for what is being expressed, and not expressed. We are making translations, associations, possible connections with what people are sharing. It requires active listening, and the pause.

Recently, Christine paused the room discussion and then stopped, bowed her head and closed her eyes for a moment as she gathered the unexpressed needs from the participants in the room she was sensing and would query next. One of the participants blurted out, "I've never seen anyone do that!" They were referring to Christine ... and her *pause*.

They were excited and a little unsettled. Can you take a guess as to why?

Take a stab at an answer. The conditioned belief is that anyone at the front of the room has all the answers. In fact, as the leader, you'd better come in the door with the answers ready. You better be the smartest person in the room, and you also better know all the things not yet known.

When the room observed her pause, their conditioned observation was challenged—and something within them understood her desire to hear the unexpressed need.

The driver for keeping the status quo on this conditioning is: *if you've got the answers, you're in control.* And when you are in control, two things are likely to emerge. Neither is good.

1. You keep coming up with all the answers, and your team stops active participation and becomes passive listeners.
2. When they leave the room, they become order takers, and implementers rather than partners in achieving the desired outcome.

Was that your objective?

It's a subtle distinction on paper, but the difference in how your people engage is seismic.

Let us ask you again, are you ready to have more of what you deeply desire for your team and your company?

It's a brave step to shift away from how you learned to do it. The secret is, if you do decide to use the five-step process of The UNLearning Factor, you'll be getting more of what you want, and so will your team. And it will happen faster and with less stress and effort. We promise.

AMP It Up | UNLearning Lab

1. What impact does understanding the intention, the *why* you're doing something have in the way you apply yourself to getting it done?

2. Ask, then listen, and listen some more.

3. What can you see yourself doing differently right away?

4. What will be the benefit to you for exercising your willingness to do it differently?

Key UNLearnings

✓ Everyone on the team has to be clear about the importance of doing what you're setting out to do.

✓ It's not nearly as important for you to hear the answers as it is for your team to hear their own answers.

✓ You become a better leader not by having the best answers but by getting the best answers from your people.

✓ You are moving toward something all the time. You have no choice. The distinction you can make as a leader is in your ability to consciously choose what you want to keep moving toward.

✓ You better be clear about what you want. And even more importantly, you have got to know what your team wants and needs to be successful.

✓ So much of the conditioning you have inherited is focused on what you don't want and will do almost anything to avoid.

✓ Your power as a leader is to pause long enough to ask, "How is this making sense?" or "What is clear here?"

✓ It's a brave step to shift away from how you learned to do it.

12

Harvesting the Gold from Step Four

Out of the fog and into the wild blue yonder.

You can't get to this present-moment awareness without addressing the first three questions in The UNLearning Factor.

Can you imagine the power and impact of moving from disengagement into the space where you are asking activating questions that stir your team's innate genius and their inborn desire to collaborate?

Yes, you read that correctly. It's in your human DNA to want to collaborate. You might think of it as being part of the tribe ... of belonging.

The fence that surrounds you from this natural state is *fear* and *defensiveness*, two states of mind that will spin you into full-on resistance.

WHAT'S CAUSING IT TO WORK CREATES ITS OWN CULTURAL PROPULSION SYSTEM

We recently worked with a team who were fearful of change because they believed it would stifle them. Separate from their leadership, the team had adopted a subculture of *compassionate service* where they brought all their life issues, challenges, griefs, and fears to work. They were so invested in each other's drama that they barely had time to get work completed. It became *As the Company Turns.* Daily updates were expected and anticipated by all the players. Because they are in the service industry, they brought the same perspective to their clients and took on the emotionality of their clients who were coming to them in times of intense anxiety, drama, and compounded stressors. Outcomes from traumatic life events.

Team members were exhausted, burned out and their work product declined noticeably over the course of eighteen months. The culture had become a symbiotic goo ball of codependency disguised as *compassion.* Our term for this state is cultural bypass. You give up the truth for a warm bath of niceness and political correctness. Both of those have the potential to become a toxic wasteland of fear and deception.

The team was proud of saying, "We bend over backward for each other and our clients." The team could not see another way of operating until we asked them the following five questions.

1. What's working best?
2. What's causing it to work?
3. What are the goals and desired outcomes you want to achieve?
4. What are the benefits of achieving these goals?
5. Who is going to do what and by when?

We purposefully redirected answers that pointed to their crises, their coworkers' crises, their neighbors' crises, and their extended family crises. Instead, we asked them to focus on what was working. To answer, each team member had to move to a different focus within him/herself.

After a two-day retreat where they got to share their own truths and hear each other's best answers, what emerged was a wholesome desire to hold themselves accountable for their wants, needs, and feelings. They committed to taking responsibility for their own actions to support their own accomplishments and each other's.

The tone of the office changed almost overnight. We coached team members to manage their personal needs on their own. We guided them to discover and utilize their personal support networks.

They shifted from being a self-proclaimed *family* to a team of *collaborators*.

[*Wonder is curiosity infused with awe.*]

Where was their leadership during this shift? They were holding themselves accountable for UNLearning what was no longer serving their team and their company. They reset boundaries and expectations. And they focused on removing obstacles that kept the team from accomplishing their stated Mission.

ENGAGEMENT IS YOUR FIRST ORDER OF BUSINESS ... EVERY DAMN DAY.

If you get up each day and tackle the balance sheet without engaging your people, you have already veered off course.

When a team doesn't feel like they are accomplishing anything significant as a collaborative, they get moody and isolate from the tough conversations. Chaos and disruption build and fester. As the leader, you isolate your team members as soon as you stop asking questions that engage their innate genius and natural affinity for collaboration.

It's imperative that your team members know how they are contributing to the mission. This needs to be front and center and revisited often. Team members are like sparks seeking a fire and an ill-informed spark can fizzle while still operating at a base level.

1. What's working best?
2. What's causing it to work?
3. What are the goals and desired outcomes you want to achieve?

The whole question-generating process makes it possible to feel safe within yourself. And that is essential to tell the truth about anything.

There are no right or wrong answers to what's working and what's getting it to work. There are degrees of effectiveness, you and your team will generate your thriving culture through the practice of asking questions to make room for truth-telling. It's a practice that goes beyond performance to a culture of shared mastery.

We recently worked with a division inside one of the branches of the U.S. Armed Forces. A group of some forty senior managers were mired under the new Command. The Command had swooped in after having been appointed and laid down their Brilliant New Plan to run the base. It would be their unique mark on a long-standing operation. Their advancement depended on this Plan's success.

Everyone knew that success depended on meeting highly unrealistic deadlines. More important, they knew what the stakes were if they didn't come through and the Plan failed. The New Plan came with a significant number of changes, all of which caused confusion, redundancy, more busy work, and a workforce who was frustrated with trying to connect the dots so the orders could be achieved.

None of the chief architects of the Brilliant New Plan had bothered to find out what was already working or how the new idea would work with the systems that were already in place and working well.

The end result was a snarl of cobbled together half-measures and processes bolted on to other processes and systems. Many of them led to dead ends and workarounds, crossed wires, never-ending loops that went into the ethers, and glitches that demanded even more workarounds.

We began the week-long facilitation starting with Step One. We asked what was working well. Engineers by nature aren't big talkers, but this group began to share. By the end of the first day, the Division Head shook his head smiling, and said, "I haven't seen these people talk so much in all the years they've been under my command."

It's amazing what can happen when people are asked what they're proud of and what they want to accomplish. When they get to say out loud what they care about, and how they make things work well, humans get excited. And this group was no different.

By the middle of the second day, after we all came back to the room from lunch, we asked the question in Step Four: *What will be the benefit when you achieve your goal?*

Hands went up, and because they were getting the hang of hearing their own answers, even the quieter members were sharing.

During their discussion, one of the young engineers said excitedly, "What we're talking about here is *love,* isn't it." It wasn't a question. He was sure.

We responded and asked another question of him, "If that were the case, what would be the value to you, and your team?"

"Priceless," was his answer. "It would be priceless."

The room was silent, they were taking in the full meaning of what *love* could do for them, what it was already doing, and how they were contributing to it, and benefiting from it.

There was a sense of wonder that the word *love* could have a place among them, and influence what they were working to accomplish and how much they wanted to make it work, by belonging and working together collaboratively.

BRINGING WONDER BACK TO WORK

An older gentleman piped up, "Well, I sure love what I do. I had just forgot until today."

The room erupted. Men were laughing at the term *love,* but they were also trying it out while they were making fun of it. We watched them become playful.

They were remembering. They began recalling the times and places where one of them had extended a job to help a teammate, or advised on a job just because they knew it would save another group time and effort. They were bringing to life the times when they acted out of care and concern for one another's well-being. They were associating concern with the feeling of love.

We watched them as they chatted jovially about how love showed up in what they were doing.

The energy in the room was crackling. The team was in a state of wonderment. Being in wonder increased their curiosity about what they were discovering. The discussion revealed them to themselves, and that made them happy. They were laughing, and they were loud! We were struck by how much they enjoyed connecting. We were witnessing a cultural phenomenon: reaching the momentum of feeling cared for, of feeling that bond via people communicating with one another.

They were discovering for themselves how the beingness of *love* promotes the doingness of it. Are you making time for your teams to play? If your response is: "We come to work to work, not play," we would invite you to reconsider the nature of play and what it affords a group of people whose shared experience can have a tremendous impact on creativity and innovation.

We never said the word *love* out loud in the room. We never suggested it or made it part of our presentations. What we made sure of was that the team felt seen and heard. That their concerns were our concerns, and that their successes were worthy.

Wonder is curiosity infused with awe. And awe is the root of awareness.

Wonder is the still point of speechlessness. We exist in a moment that fills us beyond our ability to name it or give it meaning. We are given a chance in that moment of wonder to surrender to it. It is an act of supreme humanness.

The team in that room found themselves in a moment that was beyond their ability to name it. The *awe factor* was in play. What they were experiencing was being collectively filled with the trust their coworker had revealed. Their playfulness had brought them to a connection that was beyond words. They were experiencing the desire to trust.

When teams trust at this deep level, they are connected to *all that is,* and all that is possible in themselves, which promotes curiosity and a willingness to *UNLearn.* It is also at this point where teams can distinguish how each separate system is joined to other systems. We often hear people say, "Everything's connected!" It's a eureka moment. A *grokking*—what you innately understand that defies definition. It's a feeling so powerful, teams get hungry for how they can continue to create that feeling between them.

When you feel safety and trust within yourself, you connect to the truth of all things. The opposite, feeling unsafe, is the chief emotion driving the need to protect and defend. When that happens, nothing else can happen. Your internal systems are designed to shut down anything that will hinder or slow the process of protecting and defending.

Imagine being able to unwind a culture of defense and protection through *UNLearning.* What could you, as the leader, accomplish? How would it change the way you and your teams live your daily lives?

The questions in The UNLearning Factor are built to dismantle any of your cultural processes that promote fear and distrust, so your team members can return to the place where they are generative, productive, and innovative.

Some call it home. We call it your innate genius.

When you employ The UNLearning Factor, what you will create as their leader is an Agile Culture that continually moves toward what is working *now.*

If you bother to invest the time to resource your people, we guarantee you will be moving toward a self-regenerating or agile culture. What we mean by that is, the people *are* your culture, and when your people are supported to work at their best, they will be agile.

In our use of the word *agile,* we mean that your people will be operating from an inner resilience brought about by knowing they are seen, heard, cared for. They will direct, enhance and motivate the changes that are needed as you progress. They will see where you can be more effective and will collaborate to enhance the experiences your company is engaged in.

AMP It Up | UNLearning Lab

We will talk more about Agile Culture, how to achieve it and how to grow it, in our next book. We would love to hear from you about how your investments into your people are paying off in developing an Agile Culture of your own.

Ask yourself these questions to get started:

1. What format or platform do I have in place to create a way for my people to be seen and heard?

2. What am I prepared to do with the information I get?

3. What kind of strategy am I prepared to build so people can develop resilience and build an Agile Culture?

Key UNLearnings

✓ As the leader, you isolate your team members as soon as you stop asking questions that engage their innate genius and natural affinity for collaboration.

✓ If you get up each day and tackle the balance sheet without engaging your people, you have already veered off course.

✓ The whole question-generating process makes it possible to feel safe within yourself. And that is essential to tell the truth about anything.

✓ It's amazing what can happen when people are asked what they're proud of and what they want to accomplish.

✓ When teams trust whole-heartedly, they are connected to *all that is,* and all that is possible in themselves, which promotes curiosity and a willingness to *UNLearn.*

✓ When you employ The UNLearning Factor' what you will create as their leader is an Agile Culture that continually moves toward what is working *now.*

(13)

STEP FIVE:
Erecting the Ant Hill

You will not have to waste time and money motivating
a team that is perpetuating our UNLearning Factor.

At this stage, your team is engaged, collaborating, and thinking innovatively about what needs to happen next, and what they are going to do to contribute to the shared outcomes.

Two things are occurring that are self-perpetuating. The first is engagement. The second is accountability.

There's a third thing that's going on. Your internal connection-making mechanism is tracking how the energy has been shifting since you started the meeting. You're noting it in how it feels in the room, and how connected to the truth the team members are as they speak out loud. What you may not be noting as consciously is the shine in their countenance, and that they are no longer tentative when they bring up a thought. Perhaps you note the lack of fear or trepidation in their eyes.

These verbal and nonverbal trackers are part of the literally hundreds of cues you notice on a minute basis in the people with whom you interact. Most of the communicating you do every day is nonverbal. If you think that's not possible, it's a good barometer of where your EQ (Emotional

Intelligence) scale resides. The more consciously aware you become of the nonverbal signals you send, and your teams send you, the more accomplished a leader you become.

If you believe it's best to keep emotions out of your work life, we're here to help you reform that. Your ability to notice and measure even one of the nonverbal trackers we've mentioned here makes you a leader who's connected to your humanity. And, being connected to your humanity, you are in turn connecting to your people through that humanity.

Perhaps the best news is that once you begin modeling this behavior, it will transform how you are perceived by your employees. The level of trust you can achieve using your awareness, mindfulness, and presence will create a system of engagement and trust that you simply cannot strategize or purchase.

The big hurdle here is in the power of your belief that being connected to another employee's emotional life is *valuable,* not only to the level of connection that comes from your awareness, mindful action, and presence to another human being, but also and irrevocably to your bottom line. If you believe that a sparkle in the eyes of your team isn't worth noting, there's some UNLearning for you yet to do.

Step Five is the most opportune moment in The UNLearning Factor for taking action by utilizing answers to this final question:

What can we be doing more of, less of, better or differently to get closer to the desired goal, outcome, or objective?

And then:
How will you go about it?

What will you do that maybe you've never tried before?

And then:
What's the craziest idea you've ever had that you've never felt safe sharing?

With everything you have done up to this point, you have made it safe for your team to share now.

If you want to raise your team's engagement to a level of collaboration and innovative thinking the likes of which you may never have experienced with them before, this is where you start. Consider the mental process our final question activates ... the one that you will own and implement.

This discussion becomes a goldmine. It allows your team to get more clarity and buy-in to what they are going to do to get closer to the desired result. It allows them to express their unique genius. And because you've already taken the time needed to promote engagement and creative thinking, you're going to see people asking more of themselves, as well as one another to produce the outcomes.

Bringing your team to this level of clarity will become the template for a continual cycling of effective action. This will be a process that will refine itself on an ongoing basis to the degree your people are connected. And this manner of inquiry will keep your people joined together to accomplish their goals and achieve the results desired.

This is Agile Culture Design at work.

It's when the culture perpetuates its best qualities because it wants more of what is working best, whatever that means to your business.

[*Your job as the leader is and will always be to inspire*
your teams, and then serve their inspiration.]

We've seen teams get hungry, greedy even, for deeper collaboration to find the best solutions and the most innovative methods. Human beings are built to work together for outcomes they have only imagined but not yet experienced. It's how Notre Dame was built starting in 1163. It took over 200 years to complete the vision. And now, some of that same passion is funding its rebuild after the massive fire that destroyed most of it in 2019.

Overnight, people came together to undertake the rebuilding of Notre Dame. Overnight, the seeding of the team that would undertake this monumental rebuilding started to form. And overnight, almost one billion dollars was pledged for its reconstruction.

It's the same verve for collaboration that gets a giant ant hill erected. It's why you tilt your head back to gaze into the night sky. We humans are drawn to mystery, and we long to make meaning from it: The unanswerable questions; the questions that defy definitive answers. What is changeable, malleable and wants your creative genius to shape and create from it?

And through this collaborative spark, perhaps you see something of yourself reflected.

CHANGE WITHOUT RESISTANCE

One of our long-time clients has a manufacturing plant that supplies its branded retail organization. Its ubiquitous products can be found in every home.

When we were first called in by the general manager (GM), he described his pain point, "It looks like everything's going just fine, but something really doesn't feel right. Can you go work your magic and see what's going on?"

Never shying away from a challenge, we agreed.

On the day we started, we walked onto the plant floor with the factory supervisor. We were shown around and introduced to the foremen, the line supervisors, and the mechanics. We were shown the state-of-the-art processing systems the GM had designed himself.

It was nothing short of visionary.

We shook hands with people. We walked through their Quality Control department and were shown the rigorous testing the team had developed and continued to update.

It was magnificently impressive.

That was until we began having interviews with those in charge. A man in his late fifties was the factory supervisor. He oversaw a team of one hundred-plus workers and had done so for 15+ years. Fewer than half of the employees spoke English. Most were Latinx.

During our tour, the only words we heard from the supervisor were in English, never speaking the common language of his workers. On the other hand, the GM spoke fluent Spanish and interacted with every worker we passed. He knew their names, what was going on with their families, how the lines were working, and what pieces of machinery had quirks and glitches being worked on.

It was night and day between the two leaders.

We followed suit and immediately pressed our limited Spanish into service to greet and ask questions. Our Spanish will get a room, food, and directions in any Spanish-speaking town. And that's about it.

We noticed none of the other Anglo foremen and tech support staff spoke Spanish to any of the Spanish speakers. The Latinx foreman, who had been working at the factory twenty-six years, since he was sixteen, spoke fluent English.

We noticed a distinct and all-too familiar pattern emerge. The Anglo managers kept to themselves and used the language barrier to create distance from the rest of the employees in the plant. It was a Them vs Us attitude and scenario.

The result had been a lowering of expectations of line supervisors over time. Now, in the present, these same supervisors were not supervising their teams because they had been conditioned to wait for orders from the foreman who got orders from the Anglo supervisor.

For over a decade, the system had been in place. And we could see an implosion snowballing. The supervisor interview was candid and revealing. He didn't want to be there. His self-imposed language barrier generated increased levels of frustration for himself ... and for those he supervised.

Instead of interacting with them as the GM easily did, he barked orders and returned to his office, a glassed-in area in the gallery above the plant floor. On our first day with him, he revealed that what he really wanted was to be retired and on the golf course—the more days, the better. We sensed his resentment. He felt that his line supervisors were unable to lead, and worse, didn't know how because they weren't Americans. This in turn forced him to take care of every issue. And, as his conditioning proved out, he was constantly facing challenges brought to him.

[*The factory was hemorrhaging talent ... and money.*]

The supervisor's behavior and communication style was the model for his mechanics. All of them were Anglos as well, and none of them spoke a word of Spanish. Them vs Us.

We learned that it was a common occurrence for the factory supervisor to come roaring out of his glassed-in office to berate and demonstrate his extreme displeasure. We learned that much of his anger was a result of his not knowing the systems or inner workings of the machines. Instead, he would blame the line workers for mishaps on their lines.

Employees were cowed and subdued. Absenteeism was rampant. Fights were common on the floor. New hires quit constantly. Complaints came to us in barrel loads as we cracked open what exactly was causing the breakdowns.

The factory was hemorrhaging talent ... and money.

The managerial team were mostly long-time employees, each with over a decade in service to the company, and some, as much as twenty-five years. The things we were staggered at hearing had become commonplace and normalized over time.

There was no one holding himself and one another accountable for a higher standard of behavior, typically a role modeled by the leader.

The more we dug, the more the imprint of the family-run business was revealed. There were secrets kept and emotionally charged grudges being held. Transparent communication was all but absent from daily life. No wonder the culture was dysfunctional, and chaos simmered just under the surface.

We had heard and seen enough to make recommendations. The GM immediately approved it. So it was time to move forward with our plan.

There was essential housecleaning that needed to be done that was blatantly apparent in our first interview with the factory supervisor.

The first action that we took was to bring on a third member to our team: a community psychologist, and native Spanish-speaker.

The second action we took was to recommend that the GM offer retirement to the golf-dreaming factory supervisor who welcomed it with relief.

The third action we took was to interview the key members of the plant floor. In their one-on-one interviews, we asked them how they thought the plant could flourish. Each one named the foreman as their preferred leader. We supported their choice and asked them how they wished to proceed. "Transparencia!" was the consensus. They wanted to make their communications in an open forum.

[*What occurred next was nothing short of a phenomenon.*]

Then we brought them together and shared the outcomes from their interviews. In about 30 minutes, they had come up with a go-forward plan. It was again reiterated by all that they wanted the plant foreman to take over the role of factory supervisor. They also wanted to share where they thought he was strong and what areas they believed he needed to grow. The employees wanted to have the workplace be an environment where they enjoyed working. And they wanted respect for the work that they did.

The new supervisor matched what the others had said in the areas he needed growth in. And he too shared their desire for an injection of a morale boost. He felt prepared to lead and be humble enough to grow. He knew he didn't have all the answers.

Our immediate takeaway: We had a group of honest and transparent employees. A group of people committed through their raised awareness. This awareness came online because these people were being seen and heard.

Transparencia became their watchword. It was a brilliant demonstration of individual awareness having a collaborative effect on the whole and their shared outcomes.

What occurred next was nothing short of a phenomenon. The GM committed to a multicultural leadership program, which we designed and implemented for the line supervisors, the new factory supervisor, and other managers of the plant.

Designed to be conducted over twelve months, we started with the precepts of leadership that are core to our UNLearning platforms. We built the program details based on what they had decided they wished to aspire to. And, then we figured it out alongside the team on a continual basis.

We were designing Agile Culture as we learned how the team worked best and what was meaningful to them.

One thought that stands out about how our work differs from so much of the consulting that's out there making big claims: It is that we don't *ever* have your *best* answers. And, what we do that's so different from consulting is fearlessly dig with our clients for the truest thing about their culture.

We don't leave them to boil the ocean of possibilities by themselves.

So how do we know when our work is done? The client's teams aren't aware that we're no longer in the room.

As we wrote this section of *UNLearning*, we were delighted to get an email from the GM. With gratitude, we share what he wrote about a recent event with the installation of some new U.K.-made machinery.

> We've had a team of four mates here installing the equipment for over three weeks and I've been doing most of the cooking at lunchtime. One of the Manchester team told me after lunch today, "I've been installing equipment all over the world and I've never seen employees that treat all like family! The other factories are like robots with no faces."
>
> Then he said, "I've been talking to the missus about moving here." I immediately thought about you. So many things come up walking through the factory that the *UNLearning* process has fostered and impregnated into our daily lives.

This is why and how UNLearning works. Showing teams the doorways they can move through to succeed in the ways that will be most meaningful to them.

Here's a repeat of the secret sauce we've noted: You will not have to waste time and money to keep a team motivated. All you need to do is perpetuate *The UNLearning Factor*.

Your job as the leader is and will always be to inspire your teams. That may mean removing all the barriers they encounter so they can be successful at what they have just innovated. Are you willing to do that?

More than likely, it will also mean that you hold the core of *why* your teams do what they do. Cocreating intentions that support the company Vision, your teams calibrate their contributions to fulfill those intentions. This is *how* your people will get up every day: with the understanding and recognition that what they are doing is *meaningful*.

They will motivate themselves and each other by being engaged in a continual process of discoveries and successful implementations.

Step Five will have any number of offshoots: Questions that arise because now your team is engaged in shaping the *how* and *when* of the project. The results include deliverables, budgets, and time lines. And more than any task, this part of the process galvanizes people's accountability alongside their creativity and collaboration. They now understand and can commit to what they personally are ready to hold themselves responsible for.

In our work at The Institute, we see the level of personal satisfaction rise exponentially the more teams can adjust their work to each other. The more they can express their ideas in outcomes they believe in, the more energy they invest in inspired outcomes they can share collectively.

This Agile Culture Design process has within it that mystifying ability to make one excellent.

The benefit to you, dear leader, is that you didn't have to incentivize them beyond asking the all-important question we've posed here in this final Step Five.

Taking this action to an even higher level of accomplishment occurred for us when we added a few additional questions to ensure we were getting to ever greater clarity.

Who is going to take leadership for implementing what we've agreed needs to be done?

It is a pivotal question at this point, especially if no one has stepped up ... yet ... to declare his/her willingness to take the lead in moving his/her part of the initiative forward. Then the discussion could include:

> *What do you need to better assure success?*
>
> *What area do you most need support in and from whom?*
>
> *What other questions come to mind for you to support moving forward?*

This we know is true. Your people can listen for, hear, and connect to their own experience as they answer these foundational *What* questions.

Until your people feel *connected* to your words, they will not have lasting impact. Instead, imagine they listen to you all day long and nod their heads at what you're saying but are clueless to what you are really meaning.

Here's another secret sauce moment: Turn your thinking and wisdom statements from telling your people into inquiry of your people as often as possible. Ask questions; listen to the responses. And remember, sometimes responses are silent! Facial expressions, body language, even eye contact with someone else on the team are tremendously important to observe and pay attention to.

When you transition to asking and listening, you continue to broaden the field of inclusion. For your teams, this means they get to be seen and heard. They hear their answers out loud. They gain confidence in the truth they are building together.

When people are seen and heard, they feel cared for. That feeling is what will transform your employees' capacity for successful outcomes. Feeling cared for is indefatigable. It just doesn't wear out.

You won't wear your team out.

You won't wear yourself out.

And here's what your come-from, your awareness, mindfulness, and presence have done. You've made it your job to support the emergence of your people's creative genius.

And because you've made both connection and energy channels for their unique genius to have its way and flow, they get to have them their way. It doesn't matter if they are selling insurance, or working on a factory floor, or playing viola for the community symphony. When you do this, burnout becomes irrelevant.

AMP It Up | UNLearning Lab

1. As the leader, *what* other benefits do you see as part of this step?

2. What would you say is most important about taking time to ask questions at every point in the process?

3. Who are you as a leader if your team isn't generating momentum-building energy—if their eyes aren't shining?

Key UNLearnings

✓ The more consciously aware you become of the nonverbal signals you send, and your teams send you, the more accomplished a leader you become.

✓ The level of trust you can achieve using your awareness, mindfulness, and presence will create a system of engagement and trust that you simply cannot strategize or purchase.

✓ Because you've already taken the time needed to promote engagement and creative thinking, you're going to see people asking more of themselves, as well as one another to produce the outcomes.

✓ When the culture perpetuates its best qualities because it wants more of what is working best, whatever that means to your business.

✓ Through this collaborative spark, perhaps you see something of yourself reflected.

✓ Your come-from, your awareness, mindfulness, and presence, has made it your job to support the emergence of your people's creative genius.

✓ When you transition to asking and listening, you continue to broaden the field of inclusion.

14

Harvesting the Gold from Step Five

This is how UNLearning begins.

When we look back at the transformation that occurred and continues to develop out of the Multicultural Leadership Program we developed with our manufacturing client, we're struck by what our role really became.

It was our job to track and update our own thinking to keep pace with the group's learnings and the way they learned.

They were most engaged and animated when they shared stories of what was working. Once they trusted the nature of the work, they began sharing what wasn't working and, more specifically, where they needed help.

Some modalities we thought would resonate landed flat. When that happened, we went through The UNLearning Factor with the team. We brought in other leadership principles that set the place on fire, so we dove in and deepened the exploration using what was attractive to this team. Miguel Ruiz' *The Four Agreements* had a monumental impact on them. We witnessed them orient their decision-making based on the book's four guiding principles that happen to integrate beautifully with *Awareness, Mindfulness,* and *Presence.*

Awareness – is asking what is happening in this moment. Awareness leads you to what interests you and the inklings, intuitions, links, or perceptions that connect those interests. Pay attention to those and the sensations they spark in you.

Mindfulness – postpone organizing and building a structure for *doing* too soon. Too soon is the moment you become so uncomfortable in the space between the no longer and the not yet that you collapse into whatever you've always done. Often it will seem different or new in the moment, only to reveal it's a different version of the same mindset.

Presence – is the moment-to-moment act of being. There is nothing coming in the next moment, and nothing remaining before this now moment. Being in the present moment takes practice as you learn to trust the agility and capacity of your thoughts, impulses, images, and emotions. Often you will feel presence and its attendant awareness as being in the flow or the groove of a certain activity.

Athletes use types of meditation to keep them in the present moment. Performing artists often speak of losing themselves during a performance.

When you eat a strawberry, slow down your chewing enough so you can experience the flavor and texture, and be thankful for the strawberry that is nourishing you. If you think about the strategy you have to prepare for, you will be eating ... strategy.

We learn this lesson in every facilitation we conduct, and that day was no different. Stray from the present moment of mindful awareness and what's most alive in the present moment, and we would have left the people behind. The most important lesson for us as facilitators has become our mantra:

Because there wasn't a proven formula, **we had to be willing to figure it out together as we went along.**

Did we have a map to guide our facilitation work with them? Yes. Did we spend hours in preparation before each session? You bet ... absolutely. But we never had to be the ones with the instant answers, the experts with the vast reservoir containing every possible answer. Over time, each member of the leadership team brought their unique wisdom to the table and shared how and what they were learning was helping them lead their teams. They started bringing not only their knowledge but also their wisdom. How they integrated what they were learning with their own repository of life experiences had a tremendous impact on their respect and trust of one another. They were the experts with the answers.

[*One of our major takeaways was the necessity for these leaders to be seen, heard, and recognized.*]

At about the seventh month mark, the line supervisors started driving their own learning. We could tell because they started sharing real-time scenarios. They revealed how they would shift what wasn't working to a whole new way of approaching things: such as resolving conflict; setting up teaching moments; and building a network for continual communication.

Those scenarios had been the potholes that kept the factory from operating well. And now, the team had jointly found and were implementing their own solutions. Not only did they share with the senior management leadership team, but they themselves had become a leadership team within the company. It was important to them that the outcomes they sought benefited the company, not just themselves.

Because many of these new leaders had little formal schooling, we designed a certification celebration for them. At the program's conclusion, we had 100% retention. The team members were examined on their knowledge. A graduation ceremony and luncheon were organized for them. Each graduate donned a mortar board and received a framed certificate of completion of the Program. For most, It was the first graduation they had ever attended. They were proud, and you could see the camaraderie and goodwill among them.

One of our major takeaways was the necessity for these leaders to be seen, heard, and recognized *in ways that were meaningful to them.* Having a formal graduation celebration was new for us. We make sure that our clients have had a chance to tell us the truth about what's meaningful to them and what they treasure. We ask them what they long for. Then we get busy and open all the doors we can so they can access what will fulfill that longing. For this group, having a graduation to mark their success was important because it lent gravity and certitude to the energy they'd invested. Awareness, mindfulness, and presence is available to galvanize your leadership at the moment you decide to plug into them.

What do you see as your next move after implementing Step Five in The UNLearning Factor?

The overwhelming response when we ask teams this question is "Go back to Step One and repeat the process!"

And that's another element to the secret sauce: returning to Step One at this moment turns the process from a one-time event to being a continuous improvement culture of *solution-finding.*

Here's a brief recap of each of The UNLearning Factor questions:

Step One Questions

- *What's working now?*

- *Where are you now, or have you been getting the results you want and need?*

Assuming that buy-in is important to you, notice how it starts in Step One.

- *What is it that your people are most likely to be willing to own?*

Your people own what they can be proud of and what they want more of.

Everything from Step Two through Step Five is about deepening and directing the buy-in already achieved in Step One.

Step Two Questions

- *What is contributing most to what is being done that's causing it to work?*

- *When and where is it happening?*

Step Three Question

Step Three is simply to clarify that everyone is aligned and on the same page about what is important, necessary, and desired.

- *Ask questions related to your team's project, so the team can clarify the goal, the outcome, and potential results you want to produce.*

The more you can encourage the entire team to express its best understanding of the desired outcomes, the deeper and more solid will be the buy-in. It's also the moment where your team members, who may still be on the fence about their commitment, can find their footing and commit. When they find their reason for believing, they can get on board.

By hearing everyone's response, you can be certain that everyone involved agrees about what is to be done next, and what role each team member will play in contributing to the shared outcome.

Before you reach for a stack of data points to prove they are engaged, pay attention to the energy between them. Then notice how it is affecting you.

Step Four Questions

- *What will be the benefit(s) when you achieve the goals and meet the objectives you've explored?*

- *Who will benefit most?*

- *What will be the benefit for the customers?*

- *What will be the cost if we don't achieve our goal?*

How would you describe the impact of collaborative energy in your teams?

What you notice from the answers you hear will be the precursor to your ability to start building an Agile Culture with your teams. What you are prepared to do about what you hear will separate you from 80% of all leaders out there.

Step Five Question

- *What can we be doing more of, less of, better or differently to get closer to the desired goal, outcome, or objective?*

How would you describe the impact of collaborative energy in your teams?

This self-inquiry becomes most powerful when you can practice it often—as frequently as every time you are in front of another person—and especially when you are working with your teams, where they have the chance to hear their own and each other's answers.

RECOVERING FROM THE HOME YOU WERE RAISED IN

We like to talk to people about how they look for a job because we are interested in what's important to them when they are in search mode. There are, of course, as many answers to what's important as there are people being asked the question.

We also look for patterns when we ask a question of an entire community of people because there's a bell curve that forms around the bundles of answers we receive. For example, we know that Millennials and Gen Zers want to work on their own until they need help with something specific and then they want a quick answer. We know they want to work for more than a paycheck. Their work has to mean something to the whole, to the cause, and it needs to fulfill a longing if it's going to be a job in which they can thrive.

We hear people say, "I think I found my dream job, the perfect job!" They're euphoric. They loved their interview process. They think their boss is a genius. They love the communal kitchen and bottomless snack bins. When we ask them if they asked about how their supervisor handles conflict, we get some version of, "I didn't think to ask that, but I'm sure it'll be fine. They're so caring."

When we hear some version of this, we often wonder about how much of their excitement is part of wanting to belong, and how much is connected to matching their skills and longings with the job and the culture. How much of what they experienced was directly in alignment with how much their genius would be valued and supported in their new role?

Most of us are still recovering from the homes we were raised in. Could that be you? Much of what most seek in a new position reflects how they wished to feel in the home they were raised in. Before you balk at this idea, take a moment to think about the home you were raised in.

- What are you invested in proving through your work?

- How do you interact with people who you supervise, versus those who supervise you?

- How do you experience the energy generated in these interactions?

- What situations do you feel are being rewarded?

- What situations do you feel you are being punished or overlooked in some way?

- When do you feel shame? And when do you want to blame?

These feelings are most often a product of our early life. Christine recently was hired to be in a film. With the camera so close, and the boom microphone picking up even the sound of her blinking, there was absolutely no place to hide or mask any emotion. All she could focus on was being. She asked herself: "How can I be the most truthful in each moment?"

> I walked away feeling more alive, more of an artist than I ever have.

> There was something else. It was confidence. The confidence I felt came from the freedom to be in the space where truth could abide, of living from the truths only I could tell from my unique and sovereign vantage point.

Live theatre is art in the present moment *only*. Once the moment arrives, it's gone forever in the next moment, never to be formed in the same way again. Live theatre witnesses truth in the moment you are breathing it. It bears witness to every minute detail. It depends upon the observer's *awareness, mindfulness,* and *presence* to live as fully as it was created for.

This is how UNLearning begins. You have to be willing to bear witness to what's actually happening: Not what you imagined; not what will feed your motives; and not what you wish to control. You must discipline yourself to listen for the deep truth. What's being expressed and what's not yet been expressed by your people.

UNLearning also paves the way for your willingness to forego the idea that you already have it all figured out. It exposes this belief: That because you are the leader you have the best truth and the most truth. And you're going to be able to continue to have it figured out based on how little willingness you have for an encounter with something unlike anything you have been operating from up until now.

It's a mouthful. Go ahead and read it again. Here's the challenge: Don't skip over any of the words that may resemble what you don't want to look at.

That's a practice of Awareness, Mindfulness, and Presence all in one spoonful. If you can utilize it right here, right now, you'll have a more complete understanding of how to engage The UNLearning Factor.

It is your map for getting to the truth, not just once, but every time you open your mouth or sit down to listen because once you start listening, really listening, you're going to become a witness. And when your people get witnessed, they won't be able to stop telling the truth.

There's genius in a person's truth. The genius of truth makes the humanity of trust rock-solid.

At The Institute, we keep learning about intuition and being bare-bones truthful. Sometimes, it is within the walls of our offices or in places that we play in.

Christine loves the theatre and often participates in plays to packed audiences. She shares:

> I went to a callback for a live theatre production. I noticed immediately how important it was to the theatre company that all actors were treated with respect. I read a number of scenes. Two hours later the room had emptied ... except for me.
>
> The director motioned me to the edge of the stage. He leaned forward and said, "Christine, your readings were absolutely brilliant. Your instincts are so good. We don't need you to do anything else. We'd just like to offer you the role right now."
>
> I was elated and so humbled. And the reason my instincts are so solid is because I'm willing to not know what is going to happen next. Not having to know means I have all this bandwidth to be in the moment. *Just be.*
>
> I trusted myself to just make room to follow the truest thing in the moment.
>
> The director's words affected my beingness. I felt rooted to the ground. I had a knowing, "Ah, I am seen and heard." And there's something that happens when beingness gets to connect with other human beings at that level. Paying attention to my intuition, to the signals, the messages that my body and heart and gut and brain were giving me became the work. It was *all* I had to do.

There was nothing more for me to do. Nothing else needed attention.

On this day it felt like an opening to a new depth of trust in myself.

It's what we often refer to at The Institute as *grokking*. When you *grok* something, you understand it at a level that defies words. You know it; your body knows it. Your whole being senses and feels it. And you trust that you know it's true at a level that is irrefutable because it is *yours*. It is your truth.

It's a powerful thing when you are in the *I don't have to have it figured out* experience.

Truth and trust are found when you can be present in the moment. It all comes down to *Awareness, Mindfulness,* and *Presence.*

It is one way to define being human. When your teams are not at peace or thrilled and delighted by their humanness, they'll act out in all kinds of ways. Most of it will look destructive because so much of what drives humans is based on how much shame is being lived.

The conditioning that you're not enough; you're not worthy; and there's something missing. The idea that you're broken takes over your ability to do anything else but defend and protect yourself.

Your people are constantly reacting to feelings of shame and blame from the homes in which they were raised. And sometimes the best they can do is respond to the relationships from their upbringings. The emotions generated between family members have conditioned them to be who they are now.

Many of your team members are in a constant state of feeling a need to recover from shame. The result is a focus on how to protect themselves. When your people are focused on how best to protect themselves, what else can they be focused on?

Nothing.

Most important for you to undertake as a leader is your willingness to *UNLearn*. Why? Because this approach *will not wear you out*. You won't become overwhelmed or exhausted from its practice. Because as you practice awareness, mindfulness, and presence, what's happening for you on the other side is a rejuvenation, a rekindling of why you want what you long for.

Caring for your team members by allowing them time and space to be seen and heard takes less stress and less effort than recovering from not having taken the time to listen in the first place.

The UNLearning Factor stimulates and propels *momentum* and provides continual renewal for sustaining and morphing it.

If you're saying to yourself, "Sounds good in theory but I don't have time to handhold my team." We ask you to reconsider.

What do you think your job is?

Take stock. Pay attention to what is driving your leadership style. Ask yourself how many of the tasks you assign yourself now as the leader are getting you the results you expect, and more important, desire.

Ask yourself again and again what the desired results are. Then take those same questions in to your Board of

Directors, or whomever you report to, and address them with the same intention.

What will be some of the outcomes of a governing body who has the capacity to be self-reflective? Who are capable of UNLearning? And of those capable, who are willing to UNLearn?

STEPPING OUT OVER THE CANYON

You are completely dependent on your power. If you are dedicated to UNLearning, you now realize that any of the good, the great, the invincible, the innovative that will be produced, will be produced as a direct result of your ability to support your peoples' genius.

And that your power, your reason for being, is in the *genius ways* you support them. The more you empower your people, the greater influence you will have.

We know this from experience. It's unbearably lonely sometimes and a difficult responsibility: awakening possibilities in the genius of others. It's the servant-leader personified. It requires you to fashion a matrix of intrinsic rewards for yourself that you may never have conceived of before. You will doubt yourself in the darkness. You will want to hedge your bets. And you will likely want to fall back to the ways you got it done in the past.

In your UNLearning work, be prepared to abandon the Plan in favor of the wild blue yonder. For this exercise, consider that the Plan is a map of everywhere you may not go.

What do your colliding thoughts dislodge?

UNLearning gives you the space to grasp that your thoughts and images take their endless variety from within you and the playfulness at the heart of your perceptions of the world.

What UNLearning needs from you is a reconsideration of your mental habits, your belief system of how you relate, work, and live.

AN UNTAPPED POWER IS IN YOU: TURN ON THE FAUCET

It makes a tremendous difference in your effectiveness as a leader when you are thoughtful about what you say, and the way you say it. Your words carry weight because your teams are looking to make meaning out of them. They're looking for how they can harness their genius. Where their genius connects to yours. If you're committed to making this a way of life, you are going to be open to being in discovery with yourself and your team ... all the time.

This process of being in discovery with yourself and others we've mentioned throughout the chapters in this book, is the state of being—Awareness, Mindfulness, and Presence.

Embodying the power of these three qualities will bring you back into the nature of being human. It is the beginning of your journey as a lifelong leader. It is the start of your relationship to the nature of your own genius and the willingness to recognize and appreciate the genius you are going to encounter in the people and the world around you every day for the rest of your life.

Let whatever you say be the kind of words you could live with if they were your last. *Believe* in your people. Do whatever you have to, to shift your mindset so you can *assume positive intent* with them. Learn what taking a stand for believing in them makes out of you.

Give more than you get.

We mean that with every fiber of our beings. When you find yourself looking for ways to get more than you give, you've lost the plot to UNLearning.

When you feel within your bones that your success comes through supporting your teams to thrive, you have your barometer of success because the measure of your support is connective. It can't help itself. Your success comes down to quantum physics: We are attracted to what is attracted to us, cell by cell.

If you think that's a crazy way to look at success, let us be the ones to tell you that if you think you're fooling anyone, you're not. People can tell when you are using them to gain more than you've put out. That mindset starts a chain reaction that will leave you without grace or gratitude.

And, if you think those are qualities you don't need for success, think about what keeps you up at night. Consider the difference between success and security. We challenge you to resist lumping them together as if they come as a matched set. One is catalyzed by a longing to connect, the other, a fear of scarcity and loss. Let us know when you've figured out which belongs where.

AMP It Up | UNLearning Lab

1. What is one thing you are ready to give up today in favor of having more capacity for Awareness, Mindfulness, and Presence?

2. What can you put your finger on that is keeping you from knowing your longings?

3. How would you like to access your kindness?

4. How will you recognize when you are operating from your zone of genius—the one unique to you?

Key UNLearnings

✓ **Awareness** – is asking what is happening in this moment.

✓ **Mindfulness** - postpone organizing and building a structure for doing too soon.

✓ **Presence** – is the moment-to-moment act of being.

✓ The more you can encourage the entire team to express its best understanding of the desired outcomes, the deeper and more solid will be the buy-in.

✓ Be willing to bear witness to what's actually happening, and not what you imagined, not what will feed your motives, and not what you wish to control.

✓ Discipline yourself to listen for the deep truth. What's being expressed and what's not yet been expressed by your people.

✓ Truth and trust are found when you can be present in the moment. It all comes down to *Awareness, Mindfulness,* and *Presence.*

✓ Once you start listening, really listening, you're going to become a witness. And when your people get witnessed, they won't be able to stop telling the truth.

✓ When your teams are not at peace or thrilled and delighted by their humanness, they'll act out in all kinds of ways.

✓ Your success comes down to quantum physics: We are attracted to what is attracted to us, cell by cell.

✓ People can tell when you are using them to gain more than you've put out. That mindset starts a chain reaction that will leave you without grace or gratitude.

✓ Challenge yourself to resist lumping success and security together as if they come as a matched set.

15

Now You Have Momentum. What's Next?

There is a misconception regarding momentum.

There is a good chance you have already decided what should come next. And there's a good chance your decision is based on your answer to this question:

- **What would be the next best action to build upon what has already been accomplished so far in The UNLearning Factor's five-step process?**

When we ask a team this question following our process, the overwhelming response is, "Go back to Step One."

Congratulations, you've just created self-propelling momentum within your team. That's Agile Culture Design at work.

[*The unspoken belief here is that you are responsible for the momentum starting and continuing.*]

Built on what has been accomplished, simply repeat the process from the beginning.

Remember:

There are times when things *are already* going the way you want. They are already working. And there are times when things are *not* going the way you want. They are not working!

The takeaway here is that *both are caused.*

The common sense referred to in this chapter is in your own process of continuously discovering or recalling what is causing the results you want when you are getting them.

A key to having this continual discovery is your ability to be in moment-to-moment awareness of your own energy levels and that of your people's energy levels. From your own experience, what is the difference in your energy level when things are going well?

When your team isn't producing the results you were hoping for, the unspoken belief here is that you are responsible for the momentum starting and *continuing.*

There is a misconception regarding momentum:

- First is that it is your role to have it all figured out before you begin, so you have plenty of inertia to keep you going.

- Second is that you need to figure out what needs to be fixed, and then fix what's not working to keep the momentum going.

In other words, all your energy and personal investment goes into generating momentum when it's not there rather than hunting for what's causing the lack of momentum you were looking for in the first place.

And if we may say it once more: *Do more of what's already working well.*

AMP It Up | UNLearning Lab

1. Where else could you benefit from applying this transformational **UNLearning Factor?**

2. Who do you know that might also benefit from applying this transformational **UNLearning Factor.**

3. What has meant most to you personally from the impact you've had through applying **The UNLearning Factor?**

4. Who is most important for you to acknowledge, and to thank, for all of the ways he/she has supported you?

5. How will you celebrate your own transformation?

Key UNLearnings

✓ There are times when things *are already* going the way you want. They are already working. And there are times when things are *NOT* going the way you want. They are not working! *Both are caused.*

✓ The common sense referred to in this chapter is in your own process of continuously discovering or recalling *what* is causing the results you want when you are getting them.

✓ Continual discovery is your ability to be in moment-to-moment awareness of your own energy levels and that of your people's energy levels.

✓ All your energy and personal investment goes into generating momentum when it's not there rather than hunting for what's causing the lack of momentum you were looking for in the first place.

SECTION III

COLLABORATE WITH THE INSTITUTE FOR UNLEARNING

Now you have had a chance to work with The UNLearning Factor. What is resonating most?

Depending on your answers, you have an opportunity now to engage with your teams at a level they likely have not experienced with you. And, as you integrate more of The UNLearning Factor's five-step process, you may want to explore how your teams can be developed.

Letting go of an extractive notion of what leadership affords you, and adopting a legacy and mastery driven course of developing not only your leadership, but mentoring those with whom you work, can become the most vital and valuable direction you take in your leadership growth.

At The Institute we offer a whole series of assessment tools that both galvanize individual development and mastery and heighten collaboration and innovation.

16

Our Final Thoughts

This is not the end; this is just the beginning.

At a time when decency has lost its hold on the public's imagination, and self-interest so often masquerades as success, where will you stand? And for *what* and *whom* will you stand?

From your experience of the benefits of The UNLearning Factor in action, how might you best assure that those benefits perpetuate?

There is not just one *right answer* to that question. And there is an answer most likely to be right for you: *your own.* For necessary clarity, not your answers alone, but the answers you cultivate through your people.

The *right answers* we're referring to are the answers you get collectively from being open and accepting that the best answer may not be yours. It means UNLearning the persistent feeling of the need-to-be-right, or the best, or the smartest.

This will be an ongoing journey of discovery for you, and a way of leading you can model and mentor throughout your career.

The times you have produced your best outcomes were not an accident, they were caused, and *you* caused them. You can cause them again at will in a continuous renewal of discovery and application. It is the connection of your life and work to all other life.

At the beginning of each day, know this one thing: There are only two things going on in the Universe. You are either making an expression of respect and caring or a cry for it.

Fall in love with what is wild and untamable in this world, and you are taking the first step toward saving it.

The world is mystical, unknowable. People are good.

Remember this and you will recall how good you are, and how much good you can do.

And ... we congratulate you.

Christine Kahane and *Doug Krug*

MORE ...

How to Work with the UNLearning Team

Consulting and Speaking

Speaker Keynotes

Discussion Questions

Notes for Chapters

Meet the Authors:
Christine Kahane
Doug Krug

How to Work with the UNLearning Team

Learn how to have more of what you want for your teams and your company more often.

Our interactive workshop process brings deep awareness to the distinction between management and leadership and clarifies why you must bridge the gap, particularly when the environment is changing rapidly.

Doug Krug and Christine Kahane speak and lead their experiential workshop processes on leadership development, communications excellence, Agile Culture development, and Continuous Renewal Economics. Their breakthrough facilitation work is now available for those seeking to learn facilitation techniques that engage and mentor.

They have cultivated processes that are used across the country in multiple industry verticals. Their facilitation processes are successful with individuals, small groups, and scale to rooms of a thousand.

The results that companies experience are a profound transformation in their people's come-from, their core beliefs and ability to engage and communicate for collaboration and innovation.

Our generation has broken so much that is life-affirming. We felt we had to write a book that brings people together again.

If this book is anything, it's a testament to falling in love with the world. By UNLearning anything that prevents that in you, you will begin to make it better.

We have been a witness to folks working with their last shred of energy to save what they love. We can testify that it is profoundly life-affirming. To bring that to life in your company, make sure you love what is as close to the natural world as the blood in your veins and the air you breathe.

ChristineKahane@ForUNLearning.com | 303.589.5456
DougKrug@ForUNLearning.com | 303.807.1903

https://www.instituteforunlearning.com
https://www.FalKirkpress.com

CONSULTING and SPEAKING

Workshops, Executive Coaching, Executive Briefings

Leadership Transformation

Do you have what it will take to be a leader for the future? Transforming leadership takes uncommon courage: to release the belief systems that have worked for incremental improvement up to now. Discover how to UNLearn what has worked in the past for what will work for an uncommon and tremendously successful future.

Communication Excellence 2.0: Is what was said *really* said?

For the most part you are communicating every day, but how effective is your communication? Awareness of the impact of the language you use to get your points across and inspire, engage, and harness the genius of your people is the core of being excellent when you open your mouth to communicate. You will learn how to recognize your own and other styles of communication; how to engage through a highly tuned EQ; and how to tap into and create lasting benefits from understanding your strengths, competencies, and acumen. You will learn how to increase your ability to harness competencies, skills, and your innate genius for true servant-level leadership.

Agile Culture Design™: Move from your core values to create sustainable progress

Building your corporate culture so it's healthy and self-sustaining is at the core of Agile Culture Design.

You will learn how to surface and activate core values, so they are driving decision making at all levels of your organization. When people know the value they are contributing, they then engage and activate agility in a team and company. You will learn how to cocreate and design cultural environments that promote collaboration, innovation, and well-being among your people.

Continuous Renewal Economics™: The energy of innovation

Building on the principles of Agile Culture Design, continuous renewal becomes the goal for a company invested in operating from its shared core values. Shared values used in daily life at your company become the channel to fuel momentum-building engagement. You will learn how positive momentum lays the track for continuously being able to move to do more of what's already working. When your company starts operating in an economy built by your people with their own energy, who are contributing to having it work excellently, you have the energy of innovation.

Be a Facilitator: Preparing to engage people

Almost anyone in leadership can read a slide, memorize a script, and prepare to answer a set of predetermined questions. But can they be in the flow of what's occurring in the moment, without defaulting to what they've always done or commanding the room by shutting it down with the prewashed script?

You will learn the tools needed to track the sensibilities of a group of human beings whom you manage and lead. You'll learn how to be in the I-don't-know space, to go with what's happening in the room, to listen with compassion, to guide without an agenda while delivering the content so your team is engaged, curious, and collaborative.

Speaker Keynotes

Transforming Leadership Takes Uncommon Courage

- Discover the five essential elements of your courage.
- Overcome your failure of nerve.

Participants leave with a blueprint of how to harness their courage for change.

The UNLearning Factor™

- UNLearning is willingness to not know the answers.
- UNLearn the need to be right.

Participants gain tools for how to implement the five easy questions that end stagnation and engage teams.

The Wild Blue Yonder

- What brought you to your work in the beginning?
- What longing can you bring back online today?

Participants delve into their own desires and create a Statement of Purpose for their lives.

Vision Board Your Dreams

Participants release what no longer serves their lives and discover the dreams they have been longing to manifest.

Discover and Reinforce Your Values

- Name and claim your values so they are front and center in your working and home life.

- Living a values-centric life.

Participants learn to think and act from their values with easy-to-master tools.

Emotional Resilience ... Your Super-Charged EQ

- How to regulate your own emotions.
- How to regulate your emotions with others.

Participants learn to harness their emotions, give themselves grace and love their humanness.

Creating and Sustaining Balance

- How to work with stressors in your daily life.
- How to have a relationship with your work and your life.

Participants receive tools to assist them in regulating their decision-making power.

Be Seen and Heard

- Active listening.
- The art of empowered communication.

Participants gain tools for listening, deepening understanding, and making powerful agreements.

Stop the Problem-Solving

- Hold yourself and others accountable with less stress and effort.

Participants learn to refocus their attention on what is already working best, so teams can collaborate to do more of what works, rather than continually search for and fix what is proving it doesn't work.

This is an invitation to continue the discovery, to enable your UNLearning and relearning.

The Institute for UNLearning will be your guide.

Visit their website and discover how you can benefit from their work: *InstituteForUNLearning.com*

Contact them for Speaking Engagements and Executive Coaching: *ChristineKahane@ForUNLearning.com*
Connect with them and follow them via social media.

> The Institute for UNLearning | Kahane Coaching
> The Institute for UNLearning
>
> @KrugWisdom @weareUNLearning

Christine and Doug welcome hearing from you about your success stories using the processes in this book. Share your best successes on The Institute's website. Send your stories to:

> *ChristineKahane@ForUNLearning.com*
> *DougKrug@ForUNLearning.com*
> *https://www.instituteforunlearning.com*

We look forward to working with you.

Christine Kahane and Doug Krug

DISCUSSION QUESTIONS

We asked you more than one hundred questions throughout UNLearning. We've pulled them together here as a helpful reference. We did it so you can use them as a guide as you develop the skill of being curious. We also did it to get you thinking in questions. Why, you ask?

- Because questions are a way to voice your curiosity.
- Because questions have an uncanny way of moving from being the-know-it-all, to the one pointing toward what you're prepared to discover along with your team.
- Because questions give you permission to not-know in the moment.
- Because questions put you in the state of mind of being in The Zone. That space we describe as being between the no longer and the not yet.
- Because questions keep your mind open to options from others.
- Because questions make you ripe for UNLearning.

Chapter 1 | Awareness: The Key to Leading Change without Resistance

1. What are you doing in your organization to promote moment-to-moment awareness in yourself? In your teams?
2. What is one example you can recall in the recent past where you used your awareness to change a long-held belief in yourself, your team, or on a project?

3. What is one thing you see yourself doing differently when you encounter people or situations where you are "stuck"?

Chapter 2 | Seeing with Fresh Eyes

1. What is one area of your leadership where you have felt the nudging of your body wisdom? Check in with your senses. It's most likely coming from one or more of them.

2. What is one thing you are willing to trust because your body wisdom is telling you it's "okay." Maybe something or someone you haven't been willing to trust in the past?

Chapter 3 | The Doorway to Trust through UNLearning

1. What was it that Darin believed he had to protect?
2. What didn't he trust about his own feelings?
3. What shifted in him so he was able to re-engage?

Chapter 4 | The UNLearning Factor: Your Five-Step Process and Ultimate Guide to Lead Change Without Resistance

1. If your mind is already designed to keep you moving toward what you focus on, how do you use that for the success of your business?
2. Ask yourself: What do I want?
3. What is working now?
4. Where are you now, or have you been getting the results you want and need?
5. What is contributing most to what is being done that's causing it to work?

6. When and where is it happening?
7. What is going to be different in a meeting that starts by acknowledging people for what they have done right and how they did it vs what they did wrong?
8. What is going to be different in the level of openness and cooperation?
9. How will your questions affect the sense of team cooperation and level of trust?
10. What do you need to know about what didn't work to help you get to your goal?
11. Who will benefit most?
12. What will be the benefit for the customers?
13. What will be the cost if you don't achieve your goal?
14. What can you be doing more of, less of, better or differently to get closer to the desired goal/outcome/objective?

Chapter 5 | STEP ONE: Take the Plunge

1. Can there be change without resistance?
2. How long does it take for the resistance to show up when you introduce a change?
3. What would be the benefits of being able to quickly accomplish the improvements you most require?
4. What would the value be in making these improvements without the stress and effort normally associated with change?
5. Is it human nature to resist change?
6. Is stress all bad?
7. How aware are you of the level of your people's pain and stress as a result of working harder and harder to get results like "hungry, energy, and motivated"?

8. What do my people want beyond meeting quotas?

9. What do my people need so burnout becomes a myth?

10. What do my people long for in their work?

11. How would having their longings impact their desire to build their careers with my company?

12. What do you see as the key difference between these two lists?

13. From your own experience, how long does it take for the resistance to show up when there's a change ordered from your leadership?

14. Whose good ideas are people most likely to buy into with the least resistance?

15. If making people wrong about what they have done is what causes resistance, what might be a place to start to mitigate the resistance?

16. What is working now?

17. Where are you already getting the results you want?

18. Where are you already seeing the progress you need?

19. What are you noticing already in the level of participation in the meetings?

20. What else are you noticing?

21. What is going to be different in a meeting that starts by acknowledging people for what they have done right and how they did it vs what they did wrong?

22. What is going to be different in the level of openness and cooperation? The sense of team and level of trust?

Chapter 6 | Harvesting The Gold from Step One

1. What is going to be different for you and your people in a meeting that starts by acknowledging people for what they have done right vs what they did wrong?
2. What is going to be different in the level of openness and cooperation? The sense of team? The level of trust?
3. You have been conditioned to believe it's your job now to tell everyone else how to do your solution. Isn't that how you recognize a leader?
4. What are you doing that's already working really well, meaning that it keeps generating more excellence and innovation in your people?
5. What would be the value to you if you could stop worrying about how to motivate your people so you could get higher quotas and meet stretch goals?

Chapter 7 | STEP TWO: Taking the Drag Out of Your Business

1. Do you want to have more things working in your life? Or do you want fewer things not working?
2. To the degree a person feels the need to protect and defend, what can you also be sure of?
3. What is causing what's working to work?
4. Where have you had issues in the past and what did you do that worked best to resolve the obstacles?
5. Where do you see focusing attention on what you don't want currently negatively affecting something you're working on now?
6. How do you want to ensure everyone is getting on board with what's going well?
7. How will you connect those dots?

8. What made the difference so that you are now celebrating the success?

9. What is keeping you from building a robust engagement strategy for your teams?

10. Do you believe there can be change without resistance?

11. Do you believe that incremental improvement is the key to increasing profitability? What's most important about your belief?

Chapter 8 | Harvesting the Gold from Step Two

1. Where is your own leadership style conflicting with what is being suggested in these pages?

2. What do you feel is unimportant or negligible?

3. On what points are you saying to yourself some version of, "yeah, may work for your teams, but not mine!"

4. What lie are you telling yourself to keep the status quo?

5. Are you at your best when your energy level is high? Or is your energy level high when you're at your best?

6. If your desire is to have more things working more often, what might you want to know more about?

7. What are the biggest insights for you from the answers from your people, and how do you intend to reflect their solutions back to your people so they know you are with them?

8. What is showing up for you that there can be change without resistance?

9. How is what's showing up demonstrating that there can be change without resistance?

10. When posed with a challenge, what do you notice as your first reaction?

11. How important is it that your people get acknowledged when doing well?

Chapter 9 | STEP THREE: The Answer Is Always in the Room

1. You are always moving toward getting more of something. Our question is: How do you know when it is what you truly want?

2. What do you need to know about what didn't work to help you get to your goal?

3. If you were to ask your team members today what their understanding is of the goal or objective, how close do you think they would be in their agreement?

4. Are they in alignment?

5. How close to your specific goal are they?

6. What is one indication you have right now that your leadership style isn't working?

7. Again, it is putting common sense into common practice. How will you know when it's the best time to determine if all agree on what is desired?

8. What are you ready to release in your own leadership style to make room for a culture that has your employees thriving?

Chapter 10 | Harvesting the Gold from Step Three

1. What world would you be living in where leading with heart was worth millions? Would you like to

hazard a guess at what you'd be worth as a leader by making sure, before anything else, that your teams are well cared for?

Chapter 11 | Step Four: It's Always in the ASK

1. What impact does understanding why you're doing something have in the way you apply yourself to getting it done?
2. If you believe you don't have time to get clear with your team by asking the Step Four question, what makes you think you'll make the time to go back and redo it when it gets screwed up?
3. What will be the benefit when you achieve your goal?
4. Who will benefit most?
5. What will be the benefit for the customers?
6. What will be the cost if you don't achieve your goal?
7. What is the benefit of understanding what the benefits are by achieving your goal?
8. Ask, then listen, and listen some more.
9. What can you see yourself doing differently right away?
10. What will be the benefit to you for exercising your willingness to do it differently?

Chapter 12 | Harvesting the Gold from Step Four

1. Do you see how continually focusing on what you don't want and by seeking more evidence about what to worry about next, keeps you from the real gold?
2. Are you ready to have more of what you deeply desire for your team and your company?

3. What will be the benefit to you for exercising your willingness to do it differently?
4. What format do you have in place to create a way for your people to be seen and heard?
5. What are you prepared to do with the information you get?
6. What kind of strategy are you prepared to build so people can develop resilience and build an Agile Culture?

Chapter 13 | STEP FIVE: Erecting the Ant Hill

1. What can you do more of, less of, better or differently to get closer to the desired goal, outcome, or objective?
2. How will you go about it?
3. What will you do that maybe you've never tried before?
4. What is the craziest idea you've ever had regarding this area that you've never felt safe sharing?
5. Who is going to take leadership in implementing what has been agreed needs to be done?
6. What do you need to better assure success?
7. What area do you most need support in and from whom?
8. What other questions come to mind for you to support moving forward?
9. As the leader, what other benefits do you see as part of this step?
10. What would you say is most important about taking time to ask questions at every point in the process?

11. Who are you being as a leader if your team isn't generating momentum-building energy—if their eyes aren't shining?

Chapter 14 | Harvesting the Gold from Step Five

1. What do you see as the next step after implementing Step Five?
2. What is one thing you are ready to give up today in favor of having more capacity for Awareness, Mindfulness, and Presence?
3. What can you put your finger on that is keeping you from knowing your longings?
4. How would you like to access your kindness?
5. How will you recognize when you are operating from your zone of genius—the one unique to you?

Chapter 15 | Now You Have Momentum. What's Next?

1. What next action would best build on what has already been accomplished so far?
2. Where else could you benefit from applying the transformational UNLearning Factor?
3. Who do you know that might also benefit from applying this transformational UNLearning Factor?
4. What has it meant most to you personally from the impact you've had through applying The UNLearning Factor?
5. Who is most important for you to acknowledge, and to thank, for all the ways this person has supported you?
6. How will you celebrate your own transformation?

Chapter 16 | Our Final Thoughts

1. What is the quickest and easiest way to create and sustain a culture that is working at its best more consistently and more often?

NOTES for CHAPTERS

Chapter 1
Gallup 2023 Workplace Study
The Muse 2023: Survey of Disengaged employees
Psychology Today: David Rock, November 2010
Scientific American: 2019

Chapter 3
Execu/Search Group: 2021 Survey
Microsoft 2022: New Future of Work Report

Chapter 5
Gartner Research 2022: Increase Seller Motivation Study
Virtira: 2022 Hybrid Workforce Survey
The Upside of Stress: Kelly McGonigal ©2016
*Forbe*s: Sept 15, 2019
Oak Engage – workplace culture study 2021-2023

Chapter 6
Gartner – op. cit.
Forbes – op. cit.
Gallup – op. cit.
Oak Engage – op. cit.
Gallup – ibid
The Execu/Search Group – op. cit.
The Muse – op. cit.
Predictive Index: The State of Talent Optimization 2023
Glassdoor: 2023 New Hire Onboarding Checklist
Gartner – op. cit.

Chapter 7

Gartner – op. cit.

Payscale: Compensation Trends 2022

Gallup – State of the Global Workplace Report 2023

Best Companies Group – 2/4/2021

Forbes: May 2019 – "How much are your disengaged employees costing you?"

Oak Engage – op. cit.

Gallup Engagement Study – op. cit.

Gartner – op. cit.

ACKNOWLEDGMENTS

We could not have produced this work, and certainly could not have arrived at a place in each of our lives where we were ready to share what we have learned in our seventy combined years working with leaders and teams all over the world, were it not for some extraordinary people along the way.

From Doug:

Paul Conover—my high school history teacher who opened my mind to question, not just accept—he aroused my insatiable curiosity. Dennis Wagner, US Health & Human Services/Medicare RET'D, who so naturally demonstrates the essence of *enlightened leadership.* Sandy Markwood, CEO, USAging, who continues to model perhaps the most essential leadership competency in this fast changing, dynamic time we live in—the willingness to not be attached to only getting better at how it has always done.

Gail Williams, NASA RET'D, on top of my list of leaders who started with nothing other than a clear vision of what she wanted, as she did with creating the successful Leadership Alchemy Program at NASA.

Greg Zlevor, Founder, HopeMakers, just never stops thinking, never stops looking for what's next, and figuring out how to create it. Kurt and Patricia Wright. Since first being introduced to distinctions in questions by Patricia and Kurt Wright in 1985, my life has not been the same.

And, Therese Krug, my life is blessed daily from what I gained from all the years you were a part of it.

From Christine:

The further I progress through my life, the more I become aware of how little I know and how increasingly, the world and everything in it is, at last … connected. So, it is in no small part as I write these acknowledgements that I do so with the distinct and overwhelming sense of connection to these beautiful humans.

To my dearest friend, Sylke Sharrenbroich, artist, healer, and activist, your belief in me and your keen eye on the journey I have taken to build this book from our world in Brooklyn, NY., is my constant north. Thank you for the wild artist you are, a never-ending source of inspiration. To Doug Krug, who taught me that fear is really an out picturing of the need for perfection—that being in the process of discovery, and staying curious, are the most powerful places I can live from.

To my sisters Karen Hersh and Kathleen Forgay, your good-natured humor and ability to right my boat when I was sure I had nothing of merit to say, is borne out of the blood we share.

To my book team, who has been unflagging in its assurance that the beliefs which have generated this work, are the seeds of a different outlook for 21st Century leadership: Dr. Judith Briles, who sat with me every Thursday for months while we teased apart the general to make specific meaning of my experience—your deep understanding of business, leadership, and massive good humor about what is possible by utilizing the tools in this book, are the stuff of legend. I could not have written it without you. Period. To Peggy Ireland for your keen proofing eye—and Bobby

Crew for shepherding me through the process of bringing the book to life through social media. And to Nick Zelinger, your constancy and partnership in designing this book so it works as a tool for helping leaders shift their mindsets, has made us proud to publish this work.

And finally, to my parents, Bill and Trude Carter, long gone from this life—I hope you would be proud. So much of the freedom to write from my unique point of view has come from the courage you afforded me to think for myself, and forge my own way.

MEET the AUTHORS

Christine Kahane, NBC-HWC, MCWC, Executive Coach, Resultant

Christine builds on three decades of
experience working with organizations
wanting to effect sustainable growth
by building cultures rooted in core
values. Witnessing the seismic shift
in corporate cultures through
values-driven change, she has worked
to develop facilitation techniques that
integrate EQ mastery, communication skills, and Agile
Culture-based business modeling.

Her coaching focuses on bringing innate genius online.
She has developed techniques that integrate a client's
untapped emotional intelligence to create lasting lifestyle
and workplace changes, resulting in teams who discover and
develop their own cultural veracity. The primary outcome of
which is agile culture development, the core of her work.

Christine's work in the U.S. and internationally has given
her extensive experience in cocreating what individuals
and teams need to thrive: uncovering the unique qualities
that bring lasting relevance to life, business planning, and
development. She facilitates change so tpeople can harness
their innate genius.

Her experience in leadership development and culture
shift includes internationally recognized brands in retail,
finance, technology, manufacturing, health care, government,
and military, which include: R.H. Macy & Co., Shearson

Lehman Brothers, American Express, Barneys New York, Microsoft, Federated Department Stores, TLR Eclectic, The Landmark Group, and Mercy Health Systems. In the public sector, her shift work with government agencies including EPS, NAVAIR, and numerous city and county police departments across the country.

Christine is nationally certified in a variety of areas. Her expertise includes executive coaching, change management, agile culture development and assessment tools designed for senior executives. She is a process systems facilitator and a Nationally Board Certified Health and Wellness Coach.

UNLearning: Leading Change without Resistance coauthored with Doug Krug is the benchmark for organizations seeking resilience and profitability in turbulent times.

She calls the mountains of Colorado home.

Doug Krug, Resultant and Author

The Father of *Enlightened Leadership* is what Doug Krug is known as. He created transformation-in-thinking work built around the premise that if leaders didn't cause so much resistance to begin with, teams wouldn't have to work so hard to overcome it.

A core belief of his process facilitation is that all the answers ever needed to create any outcomes desired are already available in the people doing the work.

Doug developed and facilitated Executive Development Programs throughout the federal government. Doug's breakthrough process work has been applied successfully within multiple Governor's Cabinets, including Colorado, Hawaii, and Utah. He's rolled up his sleeves to work with the top executive teams at the FBI, Secret Service, NASA, DEA, IRS, Veterans Affairs, Center for Disease Control (CDC), Office of Personnel Management, Department of Interior, Department of Labor, U.S. Marshals, Medicare/Medicaid, the National Oceanic and Atmospheric Administration, all 50 Admirals in the U.S. Coast Guard, as well as numerous executive teams in the corporate arena.

For over four decades, Doug has been instrumental in the design and implementation of effective national healthcare initiatives. At U.S. Health & Human Services and Medicare, Doug's work is commonly referred to as the Signature Style™.

He has taught the capstone course of the MBA Program at Johns Hopkins University for 15 years and is now an advisor to JHU's leadership program.

Doug's first book, *Enlightened Leadership: Getting to the HEART of Change* was published to a global audience and has enjoyed over thirty printings. Selling over 500,000 copies, it can be found in libraries around the world and is routinely used in university business classes.

The Missing Piece in Leadership: How to Create the Future You Want is used in leadership classes nationwide. He is also the coauthor of *Leadership Made Simple.*

UNLearning: Leading Change without Resistance coauthored with Christine Kahane is the benchmark for organizations seeking resilience and profitability in turbulent times.

Doug is a walker. In between turning organizations inside out and upside down so they can stand again, he embraces the Denver environment ... one step at a time.

Printed in the USA
CPSIA information can be obtained
at www.ICGtesting.com
LVHW021002230324
775330LV00036B/1357